Samuel Mather

First Citizen of Cleveland

Tasora

Samuel Mather

First Citizen of Cleveland
Kathryn L. Makley

TASORA BOOKS
5120 Cedar Lake Road
Minneapolis, MN 55416
952.345.4488
Distributed by Itasca Books
Printed in the U.S.A.

ISBN 978-1-934690-69-7

Samuel Mather, First Citizen of Cleveland

Copyright © Kathryn L. Makley 2013
All rights reserved.

No part of this book can be used or reproduced in any manner without written permission from the publisher, except in the context of reviews.

Every effort has been made to acknowledge correctly the source and/or copyright holder of each image and artwork. The author and publisher apologize for any unintentional errors or mistakes.

Book design by Lorie Pagnozzi.
Jacket design by Ann Weinstock.
Edited by Joan Levinson.

To John, My Partner in All Things

FORTITER ET CELERITER

Contents

Foreword		IX
Acknowledgements		XI
Introduction		XIII
Genealogy		XVI
Chapter 1	Family Beginnings	1
Chapter 2	Samuel Mather's Family Life	9
Chapter 3	Business Career	17
Chapter 4	Civic, Cultural, and Philanthropic Life	21
Chapter 5	The Children of Samuel and Flora Mather	29
Chapter 6	Cleveland at the Time of the Mathers	43
Chapter 7	Social Life of the Mather Family on Euclid Avenue	47
Chapter 8	Charles Frederick Schweinfurth, Architect	53
Chapter 9	The Samuel Mather Mansion, 2605 Euclid Avenue	61
Epilogue		79
Sources Consulted		81
Endnotes		87

Foreword

Over the course of our lives opportunities can arise without any forethought or planning. Such was the situation when, in the spring of 1977, Suzanne Stratton-Crooke, chairman of the Mather Mansion project, called me to ask if I would conduct the research necessary to redecorate and revitalize the Mather Mansion on the Cleveland State University campus. A few months prior, the university and the Junior League of Cleveland agreed to develop a joint project at the mansion to raise awareness and encourage community use of the building.

It was an extraordinary opportunity for me to learn more about the Cleveland that I loved. Thus, for the next six months I "stepped" into the Cleveland of the late nineteenth and early twentieth centuries. It was a bustling, exciting city, exploding with the development of the iron ore industry, new and brilliant leaders who created unimaginable wealth, a huge influx of European immigrants who supplied the construction and domestic labor, and the rise of an upper class concerned with the social issues of the day.

In particular, I became knowledgeable about Samuel Mather, who was described as the first among equals of those who had achieved the "flower of citizenship," and his family. Although few of their direct descendants remain in Cleveland today, this family left an indelible mark on the Forest City through their leadership and the organizations they created. My research took me to various places in

Foreword

the city. Through my efforts I met and interviewed many individuals who have since died. I hope that the stories of their involvement and friendships with the Mather family, as well as my extensive research, add to the volume of information already available.

Through the urging of my friend Clara Rankin, I decided to take the original research paper that I wrote thirty-four years ago and develop it into a more permanent record. This second effort has revived many wonderful memories and required me to be diligent in accuracy for this more formal record. And as for this journey, the pleasure has been all mine.

Acknowledgements

To my friend Clara Rankin who first suggested the idea of turning my research paper for the Mather Mansion show house into a book and who expertly reviewed my paper for content, syntax, and grammar. Her knowledge of Cleveland history added to my accuracy. Her friendship and continued interest in the project kept me inspired to complete it.

Annie Beck not only raised funds for Hopewell, but is also a professional editor. Her careful and thorough comments added to the accuracy of the language and humbled me with respect to my knowledge of grammar.

Ann K. Sindelar, the reference supervisor at the Western Reserve Historical Society, gave me access to all of the Mather papers. Her suggestions and knowledge of Cleveland history and its writers increased my awareness not only of the Mathers but also of related families and events. She was unfailingly helpful and interested in this project.

Helen Conger, the archivist at Case Western Reserve University, efficiently found the Mather information stored there and sent me the requested photos.

Bob Becker of the Cleveland State University Archives, where my first version of this book resides, went to great lengths to get me all the photos I requested. His interest in and appreciation of the

Acknowledgements

paper I wrote in 1978 encouraged me to continue the development and completion of this book.

Kevin Crane, vice president of technology, Nashville Public Television, my patient, ever-willing son-in-law, retyped the second version to get me started. His technical expertise helped with the alignment of the endnotes and other substantive adjustments. And his humor kept me from giving up.

Charlene Makley, associate professor of anthropology at Reed College, my daughter, helped me immeasurably with her outstanding writing and critical skills. Her suggestions on how to improve the content were invaluable, and somehow she found the time to read my drafts over and over.

To all of those who made the completion of this book possible, I express my appreciation and thanks.

Introduction

Samuel Mather was born into the privileged society of Cleveland in the mid-nineteenth century and rose to be one of an elite group of men who saw Cleveland's potential to become one of America's most successful industrial cities. Its fortuitous location on Lake Erie and the Cuyahoga River allowed the bringing together of great natural resources in the iron mines of Minnesota, coal in southern Ohio, and railroads coming from the south. This Industrial Revolution, which had fueled the Civil War, led to the creation of immense wealth and the growth of large corporations in Cleveland.

Names like Rockefeller, Wade, Chisolm, Oglebay, Everett, and Pickands belonged to some of the men who knew that the young city had tremendous promise during the latter part of the nineteenth and early twentieth centuries. Many of these men, including Samuel Mather, lived near each other on Euclid Avenue. Their social and business lives often intertwined, and marriages between these families were not unusual. At that time, private citizens gained great wealth because the federal income tax did not exist until 1913.

Samuel achieved incredible wealth in his business affairs through his father's influence, his own acumen, and his ability to visualize the future of the steel industry. His accumulation of wealth and ability to understand the forces and needs of a growing city moved him seamlessly into other aspects of Cleveland, such as edu-

Samuel Mather

cation, health care, and, above all, philanthropy. Samuel thought of his stewardship and his handling of his wealth in a religious sense. With careful thought he developed institutions that would build permanent character and independence among the less fortunate. He saw himself as a trustee for the community and its welfare.

Cleveland Iron Mining Company,
Ishpeming, L. S., Mich.,

July 27th 1883

Dearest Wife:

It was a real grief to me not to get a letter from you while off on my two day trip among the mines — and not to have opportunity also to write you and tell you how I am constantly thinking of you and loving you.

I started early Wednesday a.m. in a buggy with Captain Sellwood, and got back at 6 last Evening (Thursday). We drove in all about 40 miles — walked perhaps 10 miles, + went by train 30, visiting 10 mines + having a good time, although the weather at times was showery.

Upon my return I found your two letters of Sunday + Monday, and was much refreshed thereat. I am so thankful that dear Baby Key,

Letter from Samuel Mather to Flora Mather, July 27, 1883
Letter property of Western Reserve Historical Society

Richard Mather Genealogy

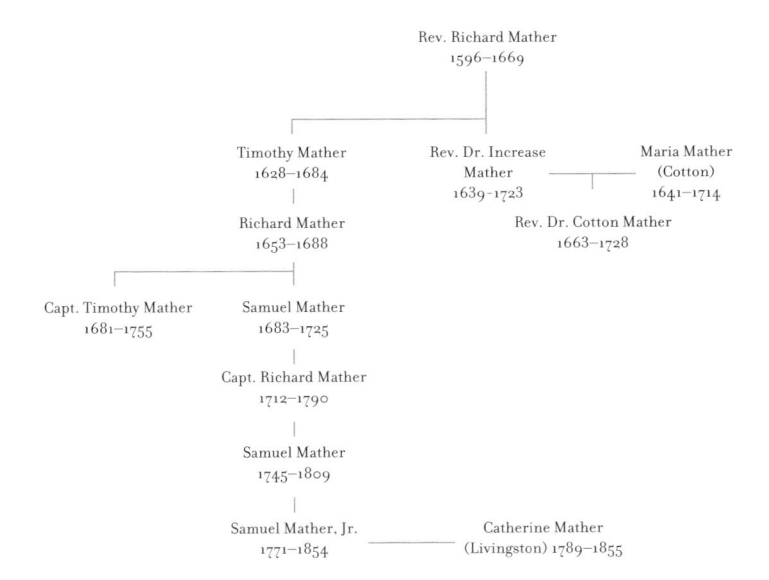

Rev. Richard Mather
1596–1669

- Timothy Mather
1628–1684
  - Richard Mather
1653–1688
    - Capt. Timothy Mather
1681–1755
    - Samuel Mather
1683–1725
      - Capt. Richard Mather
1712–1790
        - Samuel Mather
1745–1809
          - Samuel Mather, Jr.
1771–1854 ——— Catherine Mather
(Livingston) 1789–1855
- Rev. Dr. Increase Mather
1639–1723 ——— Maria Mather (Cotton)
1641–1714
  - Rev. Dr. Cotton Mather
1663–1728

```
                                                                                    Samuel Mather, Jr.
                                                                                       1771–1854

                                              Elizabeth Lucy Mather           Samuel Livingston Mather
                                               (Gwinn) 1824-1908                      1817–1890

                                  Elizabeth Ring Mather        William Gwin Mather
                                    Ireland 1891-1957               1857-1951

  Alice Mather    Samuel Livingston    Grace Harman      Amasa Stone    Katharine Boardman      John
    (Keith)            Mather         Mather (Flemming)    Mather            Mather             Cross
   1896-1950          1882-1960          1883-1931        1884-1920          (Hoyt)            1877-19..
                                                                            1887-1965

                           Samuel Harman      Edward McLean         Katherine
                              Mather            1906–1988            McLean
                             1908–1908                              (Mather)
                                                                    1913–1977

   Robert Hosmer         Grace Flora Hosmer                     Samuel Mather, III
    1910–1967                (Mather)                              1915–1937
                             1910–1978

  S. Stirling McMillan     Elizabeth McMillan
     1907–2003                 (Mather)
                               1912–2005

    Judith      S. Sterling      Samuel Livingston
   McMillan    McMillan III          Mather
                                    1916–1931

       Samuel S.       Claire
      Sterling IV    McMillan
```

Samuel Mather Genealogy

Catherine Mather
(Livingston) 1789–1855

Georgiana Pomeroy Mather
(Woolson) 1831–1853

Samuel Mather
1851-1931

Flora Amelia Mather
(Stone)
1852-1909

Katharine Livingston Mather
1853-1939

Constance Bishop
(Mather) 1889-1969

Robert Hamilton Bishop, Jr.
1879-1955

Philip Richard Mather
1894-1973

Madeleine Mather
(Almy) 1896-1981

Robert Bishop, III
1917–1963

Constance Price
(Mather)
1918–1997

John L. Price
1920-2012

William Mather Bishop
1918–1940

Lawrence Orton
1899–1988

Anne Mather
(Montaro)
1920–2005

Frank Montaro
1908–1988

Amasa Stone Bishop
1920–1977

Jonathan Stone
Bishop
1925

Lois Bishop
(Baldwin)
1934

Madeleine
Anderson (Mather)
1921

David L.
Anderson
1919–1996

Phyllis Stearns
(Mather)
1923

Thornton
Stearns
1922-1998

Samuel Mather, 1851-1931
Photo property of Western Reserve Historical Society

Chapter One
FAMILY BEGINNINGS

In 1893, Samuel Mather was a trim, middle-aged man with a long, lean face, dark hair, and a moustache. A businessman visiting him in his office then would have met him on the top floor of the Western Reserve Building in Cleveland which overlooked the Cuyahoga River, a building he had constructed for his needs and that of his company, Pickands, Mather & Co. As they conducted their business, Samuel and his visitor could have seen his ore ships arriving at the mouth of the river and proceeding up to the Mather iron and steel plants. Samuel had become a highly successful businessman and a man of considerable influence and philanthropy in the Cleveland community, and he was very proud of that success. William Ganson Rose, in his book on the history of Cleveland, called Samuel "the First Citizen of Cleveland."[1]

Samuel Mather was born on July 13, 1851, the scion of a prominent family whose roots went back to the origins of the settling of America in the seventeenth century and who left their imprint from the time of their arrival. His ancestor the Reverend Richard Mather

Samuel Mather

(1596-1669) emigrated from England to Massachusetts in 1635. He was a brilliant, liberal minister whose unorthodox views clashed with the established Church of England. His son Increase Mather (1639-1723) was an early president of Harvard College. Increase Mather's son Cotton Mather (1663-1728) was a famous preacher, writer, and one of the founders of Yale University.[2]

Timothy Mather (1628-1685), another of Richard's sons, established the line from which Samuel Mather was descended. Timothy inherited land from his father, and his branch of the family began to acquire land at the mouth of the Connecticut River in Lyme, Connecticut. Over the years, their investment in the strategic position of the land increased its value. The succeeding generations built wharves for sailing vessels and later Samuel Mather, Sr. (1745-1809), of Lyme, Connecticut, added a mercantile house.

In 1795 the Connecticut Land Company was formed to buy three million acres of land owned by the State of Connecticut in the Western Reserve of Ohio for forty cents an acre. One of the forty-nine original shareholders was Samuel Mather, Jr. of Middletown, Connecticut. In the name of his family, he invested $18,461 in the Connecticut Land Company and, although he was only twenty-four years old at the time, he was elected one of the seven members of the Board of Directors. It was this Board that gave Moses Cleaveland (after whom the city of Cleaveland, as it was originally spelled, was named) the authority to survey the Western Reserve.[3] Samuel Mather, Jr. was the only one of the original stockholders in the Connecticut Land Company whose descendants were to have a direct and profound impact on the city of Cleveland.[4]

Samuel Mather, Jr. and his wife, Catharine Livingston Mather, had one son, Samuel Livingston Mather, born in 1817. In 1843 Samuel Mather, Jr. sent Samuel Livingston to Cleveland to represent his father's Western Reserve holdings. He was admitted to the bar and practiced law from the Central Building at Water (W. Ninth) and Superior Streets. Samuel Livingston was fascinated by the discovery of iron ore in the Lake Superior district. By 1850 steel plants were growing in the Flats along the Cuyahoga River near its mouth, steamers were being built in shipyards, coal was being brought by canal to Cleveland from mines in Ohio and Pennsylvania,[5] and iron ore was being brought from the Lake Superior district. In 1853 Samuel Livingston helped organize the Cleveland Iron Mining Company, which used local capital to develop the iron ore properties in the Lake Superior region. It was the oldest iron mining firm to have its headquarters in Cleveland. A man of vision, he anticipated the future in the iron ore industry and made the important decision to ship the ore to Cleveland. There the ore was processed where coal, furnaces, forges, and skilled workmen and markets were concentrated. Thus the future development of Cleveland as an industrial center was assured.[6] In the ensuing years Samuel Livingston directed the mining and shipping activities of the Cleveland Iron Mining Company and he became its president in 1869.

The historian Elroy McKendres described Samuel Livingston as a man of medium height, stout, and with an erect bearing. He was a cheerful, friendly, unassuming man, and he held the highest reputation for honesty and fair-mindedness.[7] His judgment and views were sought after throughout the community. He was an executive in the Marquette Iron Company, the Cleveland Boiler Plate Company, and the American Iron Mining Company. He was a director of the New York, Pennsylvania, and Ohio Railroads and the Merchant's National Bank. Samuel Livingston was devoted to Trinity Church and held offices in the Episcopal Diocese of Ohio. He also helped found the Union Club, an elegant private social club for businessmen (no women were allowed), located in downtown Cleveland. In his 1950 book *Cleveland, The Making of a City*, William Ganson Rose

Samuel Mather

Samuel Livingston Mather, 1817-1890
Photo property of Western Reserve Historical Society

wrote, "The courage to venture into unexplored opportunities characterized the life of this pioneer industrialist who gave liberally of his friendship, wisely of his wealth, and generously of his spirit to many endeavors."[8]

Samuel Livingston married Georgiana Pomeroy Woolson on September 24, 1850 and they made their home at 17 Euclid Avenue. They had two children—Samuel, born July 13, 1851, and Katharine Livingston, born September 3, 1853. Georgiana died the year Katharine was born, and in 1856 Samuel Livingston married Elizabeth Lucy Gwinn from Buffalo, New York. They had one child, William Gwinn, born September 22, 1857. In the 1870s, the family built a Victorian mansion on Euclid Avenue opposite E. 14th Street.[9] Katharine Livingston Mather never married. She and her half-brother, William, lived in their father's house on Euclid Avenue. Later they moved to William's house, known as Gwinn, in Bratenahl, Ohio, and she kept house for him there until his marriage in 1929. Katharine devoted her time to Trinity Cathedral and St. Barnabas Guild House, a dormitory for nurses. In her later years she divided her time between California and Cooperstown, New York. She died in August 1939.[10]

Samuel Livingstone Mather died in his home on Euclid Avenue on October 8, 1890. The philanthropy and civic involvement of his children were a tribute to the standards he set.

William Gwinn Mather went into business with his father. After his father died, William became president of Cleveland Cliffs Iron Company, a company that resulted from the merger of Cleveland Iron Mining Company with its competitor, the Iron Cliffs Company. Through his leadership, the company began to diversify into ore-related industries. In 1907, Charles A. Platt designed William's home, the beautiful Gwinn, an Italianate villa, named for William's mother, Elizabeth Lucy Gwinn. The gardens were designed by Platt and Warren H. Manning. On May 18, 1929 William married

Samuel Mather

Elizabeth Ireland, the widow of James D. Ireland, who lived next door. The family lore said that there was a gate between the two properties, and William and Elizabeth had visited back and forth through that gate as their courtship developed.

William was on the Board of Trustees of Western Reserve University, Trinity Cathedral, Kenyon College, Hiram House, and Lakeside Hospital. His greatest cultural involvement was with the Cleveland Museum of Art, where he served as the president of the Board of Trustees. In 1933, William received the Cleveland Medal for Public Service from the Chamber of Commerce. He was home at Gwinn when he died on April 5, 1951, having outlived his half-siblings, Samuel and Katharine.[11]

William's wife, Elizabeth, founded the Garden Center of Cleveland, known today as the Botanical Gardens of Cleveland. She later funded the Master Plan for University Circle. After Elizabeth's death in 1957, the ownership of Gwinn was passed on to her son, James D. Ireland, and his children, and Gwinn became a conference center with scheduling by University Circle Inc. In 1976, the family gave Gwinn to the Elizabeth Ring Mather and William Gwinn Mather Fund. In 2007, the fund sold Gwinn to a private buyer who was interested in preservation and historical buildings.

William Gwinn Mather, 1857-1951
Photo property of Case Western Reserve University Archives

Flora Amelia Stone, 1852-1909
Photo property of Case Western Reserve University Archives

Chapter Two
SAMUEL MATHER'S FAMILY LIFE

The Cleveland Town Tidings reported that a frequent visitor to Cleveland in 1906 described it as follows:

> You will find a rather quiet city, one in which the richest people work the hardest, do not spare themselves and above all, have real consciences and do realize that they are their brother's keepers... the influence back of all this is a man of the name of Samuel Mather.[12]

After Samuel Livingston Mather's marriage to Elizabeth Lucy Gwinn, the family moved to 724 Hamilton Avenue. (Much later the Mather family turned the house over to the Cleveland Day Nursery and Free Kindergarten.[13]) Samuel Livingston's son, Samuel, was first educated at Miss Elizabeth Haydn's private school on Lake Street, now known as Lakeside Avenue. He continued his education in the Cleveland public schools and later at St. Mark's School, located in Southborough, Massachusetts.

The summer of 1869 changed Samuel's life. He was eighteen

years old and went to Ishpeming, Michigan to work as a timekeeper in his father's mines. On July 14th, he was seriously injured in a premature explosion of black powder. His skull, spine, and both arms were fractured. In the healing process his left arm stiffened, and for the rest of his life he carried this sign of the miners' hazard.[14] The amount of time required to rehabilitate Samuel's injuries was too long for Samuel to wait to enter Harvard College, as he had planned. However, travel had always been a tonic to the Mather family, so in 1872, at the age of twenty-one, Samuel went abroad in an attempt to develop new interests. These were the years that may have wakened his interest in European art. Upon his return to Cleveland in the fall of 1873, Samuel entered his father's business, the Cleveland Iron Mining Company, on St. Clair Street and Water Street (W. Ninth).

Down the block on Euclid Avenue from Samuel Livingston Mather was the family of Amasa Stone. Amasa and his wife, Julia, had three children: Clara, Flora Amelia, and Adelbert. Amasa had become wealthy by investing in Western Union Telegraph Company during the Civil War. Despite his business success, people feared his harsh temper, arbitrary ways, and biting tongue. He became director of several railroads, including the New York Central-Lake Shore, and directed the building of the doomed Ashtabula Bridge. On December 29, 1876, his life was changed forever when the wooden bridge over the gorge at Ashtabula collapsed under the weight of a train carrying holiday travelers. Ninety-two people were killed. The railroad was officially blamed, but Amasa Stone had helped design the bridge, and public hostility toward him was strong.[15] Another tragedy occurred a few years later when Adelbert, a student at Yale, drowned.[16] In 1880, after Amasa donated the $500,000 needed to move Western Reserve College from Hudson to its present location in University Circle, the school was renamed Adelbert College. Amasa never recovered from these events and on May 10, 1883, he committed suicide in his home at 1255 Euclid Avenue.

Amasa's older daughter, Clara, married John Hay, who was secretary to Abraham Lincoln and later served as Ambassador to Great Britain and Secretary of State under President McKinley. His younger daughter, Flora, born in 1852, attended the Cleveland Academy where she was taught by Linda Thayer Guilford, an educator and administrator of early Cleveland private schools. Flora graduated from the academy with honors. As an adult, she was typical of other women of that era who devoted their time and attention to family, church, and running the household. However, Flora's interests extended outside the home as well, for she had two advantages that set her apart from most of the other women in the city. Her father had stressed responsibility to the community, and her inherited wealth gave her the means. She was also a woman of unusual leadership ability who used those qualities to change and improve the educational and social fabric of the city.

Samuel Mather and Flora Amelia Stone had grown up only a few houses apart and must have known each other for years through the many Euclid Avenue social events and the business dealings of their parents. Letters of their developing relationship while Samuel was away on family business are in the family papers at the Western Reserve Historical Society. Their correspondence reflects the intensity of their love. On October 19, 1881, they married.

The couple had many separations before and after their marriage due to Samuel's business trips and Flora's vacations with friends and family members, and they wrote to one another often during those separations. Their correspondence shows that their relationship was a true match of two people who cared deeply for one another. On January 13, 1881, eight months before their marriage, Samuel wrote, "Ah, you darling little woman! I want to see you so much—letters are very well, in their way—but they do not compensate."[17] One of Flora's letters written on July 21, 1881 from Saratoga, reflects a playful mood just before their marriage, "Enclosed please find a small quantity of love, which you will carefully preserve for future use."[18] Another of her letters to Samuel before their marriage reassured him of her love, "How can I express to you my deep love, dearest heart..?" And again on September 30, 1881, Flora wrote, "I love you so much... I kept that letter in my locket & read it over and over & I am aglow whenever I remember it."[19]

Samuel's letters reflect his different moods and complete openness in expressing his feeling for her. On January 11, 1887, while in Pittsburg, he wrote of being blue and not feeling very well physically. He counted on Flora's "cheerfulness of spirit and untiring energy" to comfort him.[20] A man of complex moods, he wrote to her on September 28, 1887:

> We are all in the same category—poor human mortals,
> all of us, and at least can have full sympathy and love
> and forbearance with one another. Knowing our own
> shortcomings so well. How is it that we are otherwise than
> kindly and gentle toward others?[21]

Following a European honeymoon, Flora and Samuel lived with Flora's parents at 1255 Euclid Avenue, but wanted a house of their own. In 1890 the outstanding Cleveland architect Charles Schweinfurth designed Shoreby, a country home and summer retreat in Bratenahl, for the Mather family. Shoreby is considered a suburban home and reflects Schweinfurth's personal architectural style. Shoreby was predominantly in the Romanesque style with some Tudor details. The facade is balanced with a tall gabled mass at each end. The window arrangement is asymmetrical, allowing for an abstract pattern on the facade.[22] After it was constructed, the family divided its time between the Shoreby and Amasa Stone houses. Today Shoreby is a private social club.

Flora and Samuel had four children: Samuel Livingston born in 1882, Amasa Stone born in 1884, Constance born in 1889, and Philip Richard born in 1894.

For much of her adult life Flora collaborated with Charles Schweinfurth, on Shoreby, the Mather Mansion, buildings on the Western Reserve University campus, and other public buildings.[23] Flora's lifelong interest was women's education. In 1888 she gave $500,000 to Adelbert College to endow its chair of history. Later she gave $75,000 for the first women's dormitory, Guilford Cottage, in honor of her former teacher who had been involved in the College for Women. Realizing that there was a need for more classrooms and a place for the town girls who attended the College for Women to relax between classes, she donated Haydn Hall to be used as a student center. Flora named the building in honor of her former pastor at Old Stone Church, Hiram C. Haydn, who later became president of Western Reserve University.[24]

Four of the seven buildings at the College for Women were erected either through her gifts or in her memory.[25] Flora visited the campus almost daily, often bringing musicians and lecturers with her.[26] She invited the graduating class to Shoreby in June 1908 for what turned out to be the last commencement before she died and she gave each of the fifty-three girls in the graduating class a set of monogrammed cuff links.[27] On February 20, 1931 the College for Women of Western Reserve University was renamed the Flora Stone Mather College of Western Reserve University.

Flora's interests were not confined to education. She was devoted to Old Stone Church, the First Presbyterian Church of Cleveland, on

Flora Mather's Wedding Portrait, October 19, 1881
Photo property of Western Reserve Historical Society

Public Square. Her $10,000 gift to the church covered damage from the great fire in Old Stone Church in 1864.[28]

She also founded Goodrich House, a settlement house named for her pastor, Dr. William H. Goodrich. Its purpose was to supplement the activities of Old Stone Church, and it stimulated many social and welfare activities, including the Legal Aid Society, the

Consumers League, Sunbeam School, and the Cleveland Boys' Farm. Flora helped start the Visiting Nurse Association, an outgrowth of her involvement with Hiram House.[29] She was a leader in the Cleveland Day Nursery and Kindergarten Association, the Home for Aged Women, the Bethlehem Day Nursery, and many other organizations.

In October 1909, Samuel made the decision not to move from Shoreby into the new house that fall because Flora's health was too precarious, and Flora herself was very relieved about the decision. Flora died on January 19, 1909 after a lengthy battle with breast cancer. She never lived in the house at 2605 Euclid Avenue that she had helped plan. Flora was remembered as being frail, but incredibly energetic.[32] She was regarded as warm and effusive.[33]

After her death, one of the many tributes to her said, "There is not a philanthropic organization in the city that will not feel her loss deeply."[30] *The Cleveland Leader* wrote:

> It was her heart that was first in her giving... Her wealth made it possible for her bounty to reach out and accomplish great results. But all the while those through whom her gifts were distributed felt that the most vital element in her bounty was her lavish spending of herself.[31]

Samuel Mather at Work

Photo property of Case Western Reserve University Archives

Chapter Three

BUSINESS CAREER

Samuel's entry into business life in 1873 coincided with the Reconstruction Period following the Civil War, which had created a tremendous need for steel and laid the basis for the industry's development. By 1880 Congress had passed a protective tariff for the iron industry. The Bessemer process was creating a market for once-discarded iron ore, and new technology in the mines made the time propitious for the iron business.[34]

By 1883 Samuel felt the need to conduct business on his own. He left his father's company and joined with Colonel James Pickands, a Marquette merchant twelve years his senior, and Jay C. Morse, his father's agent at the mines, to form Pickands Mather & Company, with Morse as the silent partner. From the beginning, the company was a mining, shipping, and commission firm for iron ore. Samuel realized early that it was not feasible to deal in only one phase of the iron business, but that there needed to be a series of integrated companies with the resources to extend from exploration for iron ore to the manufacture of steel.[35] This meant the extension of Pickands Mather & Company into iron ore, ships, coal, and furnaces to ensure control of the entire process of producing steel.

The business expanded and prospered. As new iron ore deposits were discovered, mines opened in Michigan, Minnesota, and Wisconsin. In 1891 Daniel Burnham and John Wellborn Root of Chicago built the Western Reserve Building at Superior and Water Streets for Samuel to house Pickands Mather & Company. Burnham and Root were architects who combined business imagination and sound aesthetics. The Western Reserve Building was an eight-story, brick and sandstone structure overlooking the Cuyahoga River basin. The hall flooring was inlaid with Italian marble and mosaic tiles.

> On the top floor, Samuel Mather's office suite is intact. The walls of the two rooms consist of handsomely carved solid wood paneling, some of it similar to that in the Euclid Avenue house. The windows of the corner office overlook Lake Erie and the Cuyahoga River.[36]

In the 1970s the building was restored as the first step of the Settlers' Landing project by the Higbee Development Corporation.

Samuel became the senior partner in Pickands Mather in 1896 and remained so until his death in 1931. Pickands Mather remained a partnership but also functioned within the industry as a service organization that managed mines and vessels and served as a sales agency for many corporations. As the business prospered, new organizations were formed to accommodate the multiple aspects of the iron business. Samuel became director of many of these companies due to his ability to plan long range for the vast iron, steel, and transportation industries. He held directorships in Lackawanna Steel Company, U.S. Steel Corporation, Youngstown Sheet & Tube Company, Interlake Steamship Company, and American Ship Building Company. At the same time, banks also sought his

BUSINESS CAREER

Western Reserve Building, Built 1891
Photo property of Western Reserve Historical Society

Samuel Mather

astute business advice. He was a director of the Bank of Commerce National Association (later Union Trust Company), Cleveland Trust Company, and Bankers Trust Company, New York.

    The relationship between Samuel Mather and John D. Rockefeller has long interested Cleveland historians. The two men came from entirely different backgrounds. Rockefeller's father was a traveling medicine man who made just enough to keep the family fed. His mother was a disciplined woman devoted to her Baptist faith, which she instilled in her son, John. Samuel and John were not friends, but they respected each other as businessmen. They corresponded politely in business matters and charitable affairs. According to Rockefeller, they met just once at Rockefeller's home in New York in 1896. Rockefeller had invested in the iron ore deposits in the Mesabi Range in 1893-1896. He needed to have ships built to carry ore. Samuel Mather announced rather coolly that he could just meet for a few minutes. Rockefeller wrote, "I thought we could finish our affairs in ten minutes, and we did."[37] Rockefeller convinced Samuel to supervise the building of twelve ships by spring, a $3,000,000 order. Times were difficult financially for the nine or ten ship builders along the Great Lakes, so Samuel wrote to each company and asked it to bid on one or two ships. The day before the final orders were let, each bidder was called into Samuel's office for a conference. Each man received the impression that he had been the successful bidder. Later each ship builder received a note from Samuel indicating his bid had been accepted. The bidders rushed to the hotel lobby where they usually met to tell the others of their good fortune only to realize that every one had been bidding against himself. Rockefeller observed, "Great was the hilarity which covered their chagrin when they met and compared notes and looked into each other's faces. However, all were happy and satisfied."[38]

Chapter Four
CIVIC, CULTURAL, AND PHILANTHROPIC LIFE

The business leadership group also had a social conscience toward the masses of immigrants, with their variety of languages and cultures, pouring into the city in search of a better life. Many social and welfare agencies were created by these financially successful men and their wives to help the newcomers, and many of those organizations still exist today. Of this leadership group, Samuel Mather was the first among his peers. His keen, inquisitive mind probed into many sides of life. Upon his death on October 18, 1931, the *Cleveland Press* printed this in his obituary:

> Mr. Mather's attitude toward his wealth was always one of stewardship in the ancient and churchly meaning of the word. He felt that his riches were given to him to administer wisely in the interest of his own community.

Samuel Mather's inherited wealth and the success of his business allowed him the luxury of collecting art, books, and furniture. He even wrote a book, *The Unification of Italy*, in the early 1890s that revealed his "interest in travel and history as well as in the political shrewdness of Lorenzo de Medici and Machiavelli."[39] Samuel's library reflected a wide range of interests from the expected Shakespeare and Dickens to John Ruskin, and books on architecture, humanities, physical and social sciences, poetry, and fiction. His architectural books included some by Ralph Adams Cram, foremost exponent of the late Gothic Revival in the United States.[40]

During Samuel's wedding trip to Europe, he began collecting a wide range of art. Later, he formed a friendship with William Milliken who was the director of the Cleveland Museum of Art. Milliken wrote in a letter of June 3, 1977:

> Mr. Mather often came to the museum and always asked for me which annoyed Mr. Whiting, the director before me... I could see that Mr. Mather felt he (Mr. Whiting) was always seeking something for the museum. Like many wealthy men he objected to being pressed. I never did; things came if you presented them impersonally. Mr. Mather was accustomed to buy on his own and was often unfortunate in his choices. However he would take a fancy for something and ask my advice and usually subsequently bought it. For instance he was caught and amused by the Majolica Bust of a woman with a roving eye. He asked me about it and my sense of humor had been caught by a similar figure in the Morgan Collection. I expanded on my delight on it.[41]

Samuel placed the sixteenth century Italian Majolica of the woman in the entrance hall opposite the front door. Its eyes appeared to follow an individual around the room. Samuel was delighted by it, but his family hated it and wanted it moved. However, he always said, "After all, a housekeeper should have a roving eye, shouldn't she?"[42]

Samuel Mather in Cuba
Photo property of Western Reserve Historical Society

Between 1907 and 1911 Samuel assembled the largest part of his painting collection. He made a daring selection at that time when he bought "Beach Scene at Honfleur" by Eugène Boudin, and he was the first to import an Impressionist painting into Cleveland in the twentieth century. However, Samuel's taste did not develop in any particular direction, as he later bought works of more conservative painters of the nineteenth century such as Jules Dupre, Diaz de la Pena, Feliz Ziern, and Jean Cazin.[44] After his death, Samuel's heirs donated a wide selection of Italian, French, Egyptian, and Chinese pieces to the Cleveland Museum of Art.

Samuel Mather was described as austere and formal but friendly to those he liked.[45] Milliken wrote in a letter to the author, "He (Samuel) seemed a bit offish, but if he liked you, he warmed up."[43]

Behind his reserve was a man whose contributions to the city's cultural, educational, and welfare institutions were immeasurable. Like his father, Samuel was devoted to Trinity Cathedral, and he was senior warden of Trinity Episcopal Parish and a leading layman in the Ohio Episcopal Diocese. Samuel was on the building committee that chose Charles Schweinfurth to design and build Trinity Cathedral, considered to be Schweinfurth's greatest work.

Samuel was on the Board of Trustees of Western Reserve University for forty-three years, first as a member and then as chairman. In 1915 five trustees of the university and Lakeside Hospital gave $500,000 to buy twenty acres east of Adelbert Road as the site for the new medical building on the Western Reserve campus. In 1922 plans were drawn for a new medical school building, but the university was short on funds. Samuel Mather said, "Build the building and charge it to me."[46] It was completed in 1924 at a cost of 2.5 million dollars. Samuel made possible the move of the medical school and hospital from downtown to the Western Reserve campus. His total gifts to the university were about 4 million dollars.[47]

On Samuel Mather's death, the *Cleveland Press* retold a story about him and his relationship to Western Reserve University. Dr. Charles Thwing, president of Western Reserve University, went to Samuel to ask for $500,000 for the university. "Mr. Mather said he guessed he could give it. He called in his secretary and told him to write a check for that amount. A moment later the secretary opened the door and looked in, asking, 'Which bank, Mr. Mather?'"[48]

In 1896 Samuel was on the executive committee of the Municipal Association, later called the Civic League, to inspire people to take more interest in public office. In 1897 he gave a wooded tract of land to Hiram House; later he gave them the first lighted playground. In 1905 he headed a group that became the first Cleveland unit of the American Red Cross. It became a chapter in 1910, and in 1917 Samuel was named head of the Ohio Red Cross.[49] During World War I the Cleveland Red Cross War Council set 2.5 million dollars as their goal for a victory chest, but under Mather's leadership, the Red Cross raised 11 million.[50]

Another of his special causes was the Community Fund, the predecessor to today's United Way. Samuel held an annual Mather Dinner preceding the fund drive and in 1929 announced that he had provided for the Community Fund in his will. His gifts to the Community Fund during his lifetime were $1,559,000.[51] It was his interest in that organization that earned him the title of "First Citizen of Cleveland"

Samuel also served as president of Lakeside Hospital and trustee for Children's Aid Society, Cleveland Museum of Art, Hiram House, Goodrich House, Kenyon College, and many others. The man who was unable to go to Harvard was well recognized in later life by institutions of higher education. He received an honorary Masters of Arts degree from Western Reserve University in 1899 and Doctor of Law degrees from Kenyon in 1901 and Western Reserve University in 1924. In 1924 Samuel was awarded the first Cleveland Medal for Public Service by the Cleveland Chamber of Commerce because he "has lifted the public imagination to the highest level of usefulness by his own inspiring and unselfish example."[52] Samuel was part of a unique era in our country's history during which men who had acquired great wealth willingly involved themselves in their communities out of a real sense of obligation and concern for fellow citizens rather than a desire to perpetuate their memories. Even in this group he was the first among peers of those who achieved the "flower of citizenship."[53]

Samuel thought of his stewardship and his handling of his wealth in a religious sense. With careful thought he developed institutions that would build permanent character and independence among those who were less fortunate.[54] He saw himself as a trustee for the community and its welfare.

In his old age Samuel looked more like a scholar than an industrialist with his long, lean face, snowy hair and moustache. A slight man, he often held his hand to his head, half cupping his ear. His keen, inquisitive mind probed into many sides of life.[55] Samuel died of a heart attack at the age of eighty in his Shoreby home on October 18, 1931. At least seventy charities and institutions were made beneficiaries in his will. Shortly after his death William Hayward, who managed William McKinley's presidential campaign and later became a U.S. senator, wrote to Connie about Samuel:

> An aristocrat by nature and by inheritance, the hail-fellow methods of the ebullient mid-western democracy found him unresponsive. He was . . . the antithesis of the profane, red-blooded, swash-buckling of Mark Hanna, who gave up business for politics.[56]

CIVIC, CULTURAL, AND PHILANTHROPIC LIFE

Samuel Mather at the Height of His Career
Photo property of Case Western Reserve University Archives

Garden at Shoreby, c.1919. Back row left to right: *Philip Mather, Samuel L. Mather, Samuel Mather, Amasa Stone Mather, Robert Bishop.* Front row left to right: *Madeleine Mather, Constance Mather, Jr. (on lap), Grace Flora Mather, Samuel L. Mather, Jr.(on lap) Grace Mather, Elizabeth Mather, Katharine H. Mather, Samuel Mather III, Katharine Mather, Robert Bishop III, William Mather Bishop (on lap), Constance Mather Bishop*

Photo property of Western Reserve Historical Society

Chapter Five

THE CHILDREN OF SAMUEL AND FLORA MATHER

Each one of Samuel and Flora's four children developed his or her own lifestyle, but each also followed some of the family interests and philanthropies that were a part of their heritage. Their father's personal, almost missionary, vision of a life well spent was a part of each of the children's lives. All three of Samuel's sons attended Yale College, while Connie attended Bryn Mawr College.

Samuel and his children wrote many loving and concerned letters to one another over the years, including after Flora's death in 1909. Family was clearly Samuel's priority.

The oldest son, Samuel Livingston Mather (nicknamed "Liv") was named for his grandfather. Flora, clearly aglow with her first child and motherhood, wrote to Samuel, "You would be delighted if you could see Livingston's brown hands. The little face is too fair still, but I think it is getting a ruddier look . . . He is a dear, sweet, obedient child."[57]

Liv graduated from University School in 1901 and Yale College in 1905. He married Grace Flemming Harman on June 28, 1906. They had three children: Grace Flora, Elizabeth, and Samuel Livingston, Jr. (nicknamed "Sonny").

In 1920 Samuel Livingston developed the 2,000-acre Mountain Glen Farm in Mentor with a lake, tennis court, and many riding trails. He and his lovely, gracious wife entertained frequently and were famous for their Fourth of July parties. The affairs, to which many Yale alumni, including Warren Wick, a bon vivant of Euclid Avenue, were invited, sometimes lasted a week. Water baseball, a sport played in the lake with separate docks as bases, was a favorite activity. Liv was also an avid horseman.[58] William Milliken, a frequent guest at Mountain Glen Farm, often rode a white horse called Dynamite on the many riding trails. "There were always Liv, Grace, and the three children, Flora, Elizabeth, and Sonny. But my friendship with Liv ended with the death of Mrs. Mather"[59] wrote Milliken in a personal letter.

In 1931 Grace died after a long illness with cancer. Shortly after her death, Liv married the nurse who had cared for her, Alice Nightengale Keith, and they went to Europe for a honeymoon. While they were abroad, Sonny hung himself in the house at Mountain Glen Farm. William Milliken wrote that the drive to Mountain Glen Farm was the saddest ride that Samuel Mather, Sonny's grandfather, had ever made. Sonny had been the only Mather grandchild who would have carried on the Mather name.

Samuel Livingston entered into business with his uncle, William Gwinn Mather, at the Cleveland Cliffs Iron Company. He was active in the American Mining Congress, the Lake Superior Iron Ore Association, and the Lake Superior and Ishpeming Railroad, where he was a director. Liv was a trustee of Adelbert College, Home for Aged Women, and Lakeside Hospitals. He retired in 1947 when he was president of Cleveland Cliffs Iron Company. He was interested in preserving the wilderness and gave 400 acres of woodland called

THE CHILDREN OF SAMUEL AND FLORA MATHER

Amasa Stone Mather, 1884-1920
Photo property of Western Reserve Historical Society

Samuel Mather

STOUT
TAFT, STARK, MATHER, VIETOR
DIXON, PERRIN

Amasa and Friends on Board Ship
Extracts from Letters and Diaries of Amasa Stone Mather, Volume 1

Big Creek Reserve to the Cleveland MetroParks. Later he gave 316 acres in Mentor near his farm to the Holden Arboretum. He died on September 11, 1960.[60]

Samuel and Flora Mather's second child was Amasa Stone Mather, named after Flora's father. Amasa was clearly an intellectually gifted child showing many interests, including the natural world and literature. Amasa attended University School where he exhibited a flair for the stage. He was a member of their Dramatic Club and appeared in a play called "Freezing Your Mother-in-Law or a Delightful Frost" with Warren Wick.[61] After graduating in 1903, his interest in theater continued and in 1916 Amasa was the hero in the film "Perils of Society" which was shown as a benefit for the Western Reserve Historical Society.

Following his graduation from Yale in 1907, Amasa and three friends took a one-and-a-half year trip around the world, stopping to hunt big game in British East Africa. Amasa kept an extensive diary and notes of his travels. These papers reflect an intelligent and intellectual young man, full of curiosity about the world and the individuals he met during his trip. They also reveal a man of natural leadership and ability to take charge in unusual circumstances. The family was so interested in Amasa's letters that Samuel asked him to prepare the papers to be published. The result is a two-volume series of Amasa's story abroad. The books were printed privately for family and friends.[62]

Amasa's writings reflect a man of his time and the culture of the white big-game hunter in third-world countries. On one occasion, from Dak Bungalow (post house for travelers) near Fatehpu in Sikki (Sikri), India, he handled an impromptu need for leadership with ease and confidence. He described himself as "Protector of the Poor" when the headman of a small village of huts asked him to be a judge of a situation in which a theft had been committed. The headman, seeing Amasa as a sahib, approached and asked

> the representative of the superior race to act as a judge. At first I was inclined to refuse, as was in a hurry, but I reflected that any Englishman would do it, as they feel bound to always see that the natives get fair play, and that were I to refuse, it would detract from the dignity and position of the white man.[63]

Amasa was seated on a chair while the head man with his wand of office and his Shikari, a native hunter who serves as a guide, and who knew a little English, stood at his left.

> I wasn't able to understand too much of the proceedings, but listened gravely to a good deal of talk. I gathered that somebody had stolen something. I therefore rapped for silence, and delivered my verdict of twenty stripes. All bowed in assent, and two sturdy henchmen dragged forward the delinquent. Here I dramatically stretched out the hand-of-mercy, and remitted the punishment on the condition that the thief should restore what he had stolen. This he immediately did, and with tears in his eyes crept forward and kissed my foot in token of thanks and submission to the white sahib's decision. I suppose I should have given them all a good licking, but really hadn't the heart to, as they seem like so many children.[64]

While on one of his big game hunts on the Keenyaleela River, he wrote:

> I administered twenty lashes to Jeramba, my second gun boy, for carelessness, disobedience and sulkiness (only

today he had broken the edge of our best axe by using it to chop bones with, contrary to orders). Very dirty in camp tonight.[65]

The group of young men with Amasa sometimes diverged from each other in their travels in Africa and India. On March 23, 1908, Amasa received a telegram in Bombay saying that their friend Gilbert Stark was very sick with a fever in Mangalore, a town on the southwestern coast of India. The town was known to be where the famous Malabar pirates had stayed. After a two-and-a-half day journey by rail, they reached Mangalore only to find out that Gil had died an hour before. He had been overcome by smallpox and, unlike Amasa, he apparently had not been vaccinated. Amasa arranged for a burial and service at the grave. However, Gil's parents requested that they cremate their son and have his ashes sent home. Amasa honored the request and bought a small silver casket for the ashes which were returned to his family along with Gil's personal possessions. He settled all of the monies due for the care of Gil and wrote letters of acknowledgements and thanks to all those who had cared for his friend.[66]

Upon his return, Amasa was invited to the White House to discuss his trip with President Theodore Roosevelt.[67] The invitation was probably extended because of his father's reputation and influence and because President Roosevelt was a big game hunter himself. Some of Amasa's trophies hang in the Cleveland Museum of Natural History. His other interests included foxhunting and sailing.[68]

On December 2, 1911, Amasa married Katharine Boardman Hoyt (known as "Kitty"), whose father, James Humphrey Hoyt, was a steel and shipping lawyer and the marine lawyer for Pickands Mather & Co.[69] Kitty Mather was the first president of the Junior League of Cleveland from 1912 to 1914 and served again as president from

1920 to 1921. Kitty's friend, Marie Wing, remembered her conducting Junior League meetings at the Mather house at 2605 Euclid Avenue while pregnant with her first child.[70] Amasa and Kitty lived at the Mather Mansion until moving to 10723 East Boulevard. They had two children, Katharine and Samuel II.

When Amasa was seven years old, his father had named a mining town after him on the Upper Peninsula of Michigan, anticipating his future in mining. Amasa entered his father's business at Pickands Mather & Co. and was made head of the Pickands Mather Iron Ore Department. When visiting the mines Amasa always wore a battered hat and mixed easily with the miners. He was tall and had a certain warmth and purpose to his personality. He was concerned with increasing safety measures in the mines and with the expansion and development of the industry.[71] However, tragedy struck in 1920 while he was waiting to attend the International Red Cross Conference with his father who was a delegate to the conference. Amasa contracted influenza and died on February 9, 1920 at the age of thirty-five. At his death his family published some of his verses and songs in a book and mourned the loss of their talented and beloved Amasa.

Constance Mather (known as "Connie"), the third child and only daughter of Samuel and Flora, attended Hathaway Brown and Briarcliff Schools. Connie was described as charming, reserved, like her father, and as loving poetry and travel.[72] Her social debut was made at Shoreby. Marie Remington Wing, a lawyer and close friend of Connie, frequently spent the night with her at the Mather house. One snowy night in 1913 after leaving the room several times rather mysteriously to make phone calls, Connie confided to Marie that she was about to become engaged to Dr. Robert Bishop, Jr. He was on call at Sunny Acres Hospital and, given the bad weather, she was concerned about him.[73]

Letters from their courtship describe their relationship. Robert wrote to Connie on October 7, 1913:

> and Pal [his name for Connie]–Dear–did you remember to wear the violets and did they comfort you a wee bit and tell you every step of the way that I love you—love you . . these next few months should be our very own—in which we have to know each other. . .so let's keep it to ourselves for a long, long time and explore this new found heaven of ours.[74]

Connie's wedding to Robert took place at the Mather home at 2605 Euclid Avenue on December 5, 1914. Marie and Katharine Brooks were two of Connie's bridesmaids. Marie remembered Connie coming down the stairs on her father's arm the day of the wedding. The *Cleveland Town Topics* reported enthusiastically about the society wedding for 700 guests:

> The Bride is one of the loveliest girls of her set and in her wedding gown of white satin, she was as beautiful. . . .
> Her gown . . . was trimmed with rose point lace and had been worn by her mother, the late Flora Stone Mather, on her wedding gown. . . . So tasteful is the Mather home throughout, that to attempt to decorate it, in the ordinary meaning of the word, meant to detract from its beauty, for every part of the room is a decoration in itself.
>
> Simple decorations of tall vases of yellow chrysanthemums were used in the large entrance hall and throughout the house.[75]

Connie and Robert spent the first years of their marriage living in the Mather Mansion and had four sons: Robert Hamilton III,

William Mather, Amasa Stone, and Jonathan Stone. As was the case for many families at that time, some of their sons fought in World War II. Their second son, William Mather Bishop, was so anxious to be part of the war effort that he joined the United Kingdom Air Liaison Mission in Canada. Bill was killed when his freighter was torpedoed by a German U-Boat in the Atlantic Ocean while on his way to Europe in August 1941. Confirmation of his death, "lost at sea," was sent to his distraught parents after a delay of several weeks. A memorial service for Bill was held in Gates Mills, Ohio at St. Christopher's Church.[76]

Robert Bishop was well known for his professional dedication to eradicating tuberculosis. After organizing the Department of Tuberculosis for the city in 1917, he became Commissioner of Health for Cleveland. He expanded and modernized Sunny Acres, a hospital dedicated to caring for patients with that disease. Robert was director of Lakeside Hospital for twelve years and was director of University Hospitals from 1931 to 1937.[77] Robert and Connie's home, Arrowhead Farm in Novelty, Ohio, was the site of the 1973 Junior League Decorator Show House.

Connie's civic interests involved her mostly in health and education. She was president of the Family Health Association, a trustee of the Cleveland Foundation on its distribution committee, a member of the Advisory Council of Flora Stone Mather College, and trustee of the Phillis Wheatley Association. In 1964 Miami University of Oxford, Ohio gave her an honorary degree.[78] She died on December 23, 1969.

The youngest child of Samuel and Flora Mather was Philip Richard, born on May 19, 1894. After Flora died, Connie helped take over the raising of Philip. Like his brothers, he graduated from University School (1912) and Yale University (1916). Philip has been described by those who knew him as tall, athletic, very sensitive, interested in people, forward looking, and philanthropic.[79]

In a letter from Keewaydin Camp on August 14, 1911, Philip wrote to his sister, "I have been having a fine time, heightened by the fact that a letter and a couple of postals have come from you." He was delighted that he was among a few selected to the Keewaydin Gigitowin society which meant he had to run errands for the older boys when they called, "Oh, neophyte."[80] On January 5, 1912 he wrote to Connie from Yale:

> I had a little attack of homesickness when I first got here. I had such a splendid time at home, but I guess I am all right now. Tell Father how sorry I was that he didn't get down to see me off. He said he intended to…Give my best love to father, Am Camasal and Katherine, Liv, Grace, Uncle Will and Aunt Kate when you see them, but remember that I love you an awful lot too, your mostest lovingist brother, Phidy.[81]

During Flora's illness and death, the family had not shared many details with Phil. On October 20, 1912 in a letter to Connie from Yale, he expressed his concern about his mother's illness affecting other members of the family:

> Just exactly what did Mother die of? I never had heard but a vague idea of lung trouble. Have any near relatives been subject to consumption or heart disease or rheumatism or cancer or disease of kidneys or nervous disorder? Have I ever had inflammatory rheumatism? I have a vague impression of it when very young.[82]

Philip was a captain in the field artillery in World War I. On June 19, 1918, he wrote to Amasa as he was starting in the Army:

> I feel, somehow, awfully certain that we will get back

again all right, or that I will anyhow. Maybe that is just
because I haven't been up against the real thing yet.
Even now in this imminent danger of submarines, I feel
perfectly safe.[83]

At Christmas in 1922 while overseas, he wrote to Connie:

You are the only real Santa Claus there is. Your splendid
long letters with its lists of gifts were only a faint hint of
the glorious treasures contained in the large box which
arrived safely.[84]

Following the end of the war, he joined his father's business at Pickands Mather & Company. However, Philip loved horses and squash and was probably more of a scholar than a businessman.[85] He married Madeleine Almy on August 17, 1917. It was a family custom to commemorate important family events with a poem. This poem, dedicated to Philip and Madeleine, was probably written by Amasa:

Her name was Almy last night.
Almy the night before;
But she's going to be Mather all right
And Mather forever more;
Tomorrow she'll be married just as tight as tight can be

And an honest-to-goodness member of the Mather families:
Glorious! Glorious!
Isn't this simp-u-lee uproarious?
We're all just silly as silly and happy as can be.
For tomorrow is the Wedding Day![86]

Philip and Madeleine had four daughters: Constance, Anne, Madeleine, and Phyllis. When Constance, known as "Connie," was about four years old, the entire family lived in the Mather Mansion for a year until they moved to their permanent home at 2521 Fairmount Boulevard in Cleveland Heights.[87]

Philip belonged to a social group of men, most of whom had graduated from Yale. This group, known as the "Down and Outward Club" or "The Gang," included David Ford, Charles Burke, and Alexander Robinson, among others. Parties were often held at homes of those who had third-floor ballrooms. One evening the party was at the Mather's house on Euclid Avenue, and Philip was the host. However, there was no piano on the third floor for the orchestra, so about eight members of The Gang carried the piano from the drawing room on the first floor, up the wide staircase, and into the ballroom on the third floor. Alexander Robinson recalled that they never found out how Samuel Mather had the piano returned to the first floor after the party.[88]

As their girls grew up and married, Philip, Madeleine, and the Mather family faced the issue of racially mixed marriage. Connie wrote to her niece Annie Mather on June 5, 1950 that Annie was marrying a "colored" person (Frank) who appears "an attractive and likeable person." Connie's opinions were mixed in her wanting to accept the marriage and yet having concerns about the implications in the society at that time. She wrote, "We do modify 'pursuit of happiness' by saying that one does not carry this to the extent of infringing on the rights of others to happiness."[89] A few days later, Connie wrote to Philip and Madeleine about her thoughts on the details of the marriage ceremony. "It is our thought, Phil, that you should give her away—in recognition of her freedom of choice and of your desire as a parent not to be an agent of disunion." Regarding the place for the marriage ceremony, Connie felt that the marriage should not take place in Frank's sister's apartment in New York City, but "on some neutral ground where it can never be said that *her* (Annie's family) allowed *his* family to do the job."[90]

Samuel Mather

After he retired from Pickands Mather & Co. in 1936, Philip left Cleveland and settled in Boston. He became active in and was later made chairman of the board of the American Social Health Association. Philip was honored for twenty-five years of volunteer service to that organization. He was a director of the National Health Council and a trustee of Kenyon College. In 1963 Philip was honored by University School as its outstanding alumnus of that year.[91] He was also a director of Cleveland Cliffs Iron Company, a trustee of the Welfare Federation of Greater Cleveland, and a trustee of Goodrich Settlement House. Philip was a secretary of the old Cleveland Association for Criminal Justice and a leader in the Community Fund. In May 1973 he made a contribution for a professorship in the name of his mother at Case Western Reserve University on what turned out to be his last visit to Cleveland. Philip died just a few months later on September 19, 1973.[92]

Today there are no descendants left in Cleveland who carry the Mather name. However, there are still direct descendants who live there and make their influence felt in the city. The fourth generation, S. Sterling McMillan III (Ted) and his wife, Judith, live in a house built on the property of Samuel Livingston Mather. The fifth generation, Sandy McMillan and his wife, Claire, have restored Liv's home on the same property and reside there today.

Chapter Six
CLEVELAND AT THE TIME OF THE MATHERS

From the beginning, when Samuel Mather, Jr. first invested in the Connecticut Land Company, the Mathers were involved with Cleveland history. As the city grew, so did their involvement. In the mid-nineteenth century Cleveland changed from a small center of local trade to a sprawling metropolis of over 500,000 people.[93] Its geographical location, combined with the Minnesota and Michigan iron ore deposits, Pennsylvania coal, and a surplus of labor provided the right ingredients for its massive industrialization. The rush of immigrants into the city following the Civil War dramatically changed the religious and social homogeneity of the community.[94] The industrial growth in Cleveland increased so rapidly that its harbor facilities soon became inadequate. The year 1896 found Samuel Mather testifying before the House of Representatives Committee on Rivers and Harbors in Washington, D.C. on the need for enlarging the Cleveland shipping port.[95]

Cleveland never developed a subway or elevated train system, which delayed the development of the suburbs until the 1920s when automobile use became widespread. However, when the electric streetcar was introduced in the 1890s, residential dispersal within the city itself became possible. Between 1870 and 1915 the city became more tightly organized. A solid industrial belt developed for several miles along the length of the Cuyahoga River Valley. Lower Euclid and Superior Avenues and East 9th Street became the main commercial and financial district for the city. The diversity and locales of the population began to change. As more immigrants arrived and settled on the near east side, the native Cleveland population began to move toward the suburbs.[96] In the late nineteenth century the black Clevelanders lived in the Central Avenue district, but by 1910 their population had expanded between Central and Euclid Avenue, and to the south and east along Scovill and Woodland Avenues. Blacks were prevented from moving to the north by Euclid Avenue and its wealthy section, to the south and west by the Cuyahoga River with its industrial zone, and on the east side by East 55th Street, due to newly arrived European emigrants who had settled on the near east side.

The wealthier native white Clevelanders then began to move out of this area.[97] Many of them moved beyond East 55th Street to the expensive development between Hough and Euclid Avenue. By 1910 Italian immigrants in Cleveland were more separated from the native white elements than were the blacks. The city's Hungarian, Russian, and Romanian immigrant communities also had a fairly high degree of isolation. Prior to World War I, almost seventy-five percent of Cleveland's population was foreign born.[98] The city had been increasing in size, wealth, and importance, but this contrasted significantly with the poor housing conditions concurrent with an exploding population. Most citizens worked twelve hours a day. Sanitation was poor due to inadequate sewage treatment, and the typhoid rate in Cleveland was three times more than that of Manhattan and Brooklyn combined.[99]

In the late nineteenth century a few private organizations formed to help the poor and needy. Examples of these were the Cleveland Bethel Union in 1867 and the Society for Organized Charity in 1881. Despite such recognition of the environmental causes of poverty, many in the community continued to fear that giving relief destroyed the moral fiber of the recipients unless it was "earned by hard working circumstances." The general feeling of the middle class, who now saw their community inundated with foreigners, was that poverty was the result of shiftlessness and laziness and not due to external circumstances.[100]

Political reform was largely prevented by blind allegiance to the Democratic and Republican parties. The immigrants looked to local ward bosses for political advice and employment. By 1900 the mood of the city's leaders was changing. This was reflected in a speech given by Samuel Mather to the Chamber of Commerce. In his address "The Businessman—His Responsibilities as a Citizen," Samuel said he had grown less attentive to his duties as a citizen in the last twenty years. He felt the businessmen should blame themselves for allowing bossism and ward politicians complete control. He suggested that businessmen pay less attention to their jobs and more to serving the city.[101] Tom L. Johnson, known as the "reform mayor" served from 1901 to 1909, during which time there was increased interest in civic improvement and political reforms in such areas as sewer systems, mass transportation, roads, and housing codes.[102]

In 1900 Bethel Associated Charities formed the Associated Charities to deal primarily with individual cases of the needy and disabled and only secondarily with social action.[103] It worked with such agencies as the Mather College Department of Household Administration to help families with their budgets in ethnic neighborhoods such as the Harvard-Broadway area.[104] By 1909 there were nine settlement houses and neighborhood centers in Cleveland, including Goodrich House, which Flora Stone Mather had established in 1896. These institutions provided services in recreation, education, and character building.[105]

In 1912 Cleveland's civic leaders created the City Club to act as a clearinghouse of ideas for important issues. It was a place where men of all parties, creeds, and races could meet to discuss ideas for "improvement of political, social, and economic conditions of the entire community."[106] Amasa Stone Mather and Robert Bishop Jr. were on the first Board of Directors.

In 1916 Amasa Mather headed a subcommittee for the Cleveland Chapter of the American Red Cross to determine relief needs and administer relief for trouble along the Mexican border. He called on Associated Charities to assume the task, and they agreed.[107] By 1919 Samuel Mather, as chairman of Cleveland's Red Cross War Council, suggested the organization continue its efforts in peacetime. The Cleveland Community Council was created to combine fundraising for the Welfare Federation Budget Committee made up of seventy-seven agencies and a fund of $500,000 for a possible disaster or epidemic.[108] In later years Samuel's willingness to commit himself to Cleveland's problems involved him in national issues as well. In 1928 Samuel accepted a seat on the Board of the Association against the Prohibition Amendment, a gesture that indicated his views on that subject.[109] He was also asked by President Herbert Hoover to attend a meeting of an unemployment committee in Washington to discuss reducing the national unemployment.

Samuel and his family's relentless and sincere interest in social and civic welfare resulted in the establishment of, or involvement in, most of the organizations created in Cleveland during the late nineteenth and early twentieth centuries. Their efforts and interest resulted in a legacy that continues today.

Chapter Seven
SOCIAL LIFE OF THE MATHER FAMILY ON EUCLID AVENUE

The Mather family was intimately involved in that period of Cleveland history known as the Euclid Avenue Era. Most of Samuel's home life was spent in residences on Euclid Avenue beginning with his first years in his parents' home at 17 Euclid Avenue and ending with the mansion at 2605 Euclid Avenue. As a married couple, Samuel and Flora lived in the Amasa Stone house at 1265 Euclid Avenue. One of the most exciting, romantic, and materialistic eras in Cleveland history is that of the Golden Age of Euclid Avenue from approximately 1850 to 1925. Its reputation has risen to almost mythic proportions of the very carefree life of the very wealthy homeowners. The families knew each other, entertained with lavish parties, and often intermarried.

Euclid Avenue received its name from the township of Euclid through which it passed. A disagreement had developed between Moses Cleaveland and his surveyors. He gave the surveyors the land in reparation, and they named it Euclid after the Greek mathematician.[110] The street was not part of Moses Cleaveland's first survey. It was surveyed in 1816 and added onto Public Square.[111] The roadway

Painting by F.B. Egan, Sleigh Racing on Euclid Avenue, *with Mansions of T. Sterling Beckwith and Randall H. Wade in the Background*
Property of Western Reserve Historical Society

was flanked on the north and south by ridges that produced excellent building sites. The ridge on the north side provided a view of Lake Erie, increasing the desirability of that side of the street. A natural rivalry sprang up between the two sides; those on the north side called themselves the "nabobs," and those on the south side were the "bobs." On the north side there were "estates" and on the south side there were "houses and lots."[112]

The merchant princes of the nineteenth century whose hard work, bold ventures, and wise investments produced many of the great innovations of the multifaceted twentieth century were attracted to Euclid Avenue. Successful men such as John D. Rockefeller, Jeptha Wade Sr., Leonard Hanna, William Chisholm Sr., Amasa Stone, Worcester Warner, Ambrose Swasey, and many others built large and impressive homes that reflected their successes.[113] The homes were set back from the sidewalk with a large expanse of lawn in front, decorated with cast-iron animals and huge flower urns. Smooth driveways carried coaches and carriages to the front steps of the imposing residences. Many mansions were in the Victorian tradition with gables, towers, high-ceilinged rooms and tall windows. There were also Greek revival styles with high pillars, Gothic, Colonial, as well as houses that defied classification.[114] The most elegant of these homes lay on "Millionaires' Row," loosely defined as those homes that were built between East 9th Street and East 40th Street. Toward the west end was the business district and the beginning of the tall buildings. Beyond East 40th Street, Euclid Avenue had the sleepy tree-lined look of a small town street.[115]

In keeping with the beauty of the street and the influence of the homeowners, the streetcars coming east from Public Square on Euclid Avenue were routed south on East Ninth Street (Erie) to Prospect Avenue up to East 40th Street (Case Avenue) where they turned north again and then proceeded east on Euclid Avenue. The avenue was famous for its horse and sleigh races on late winter afternoons on the weekends. Beginning in 1867,

> the races were so popular that the city council suspended its six-mile-per-hour speed limit during the winter season and red flags went up at 9th/40th Street to suspend public travel on the two-mile course.[116]

In the summer the young gentry of Euclid and Prospect drove their spirited teams across town to the Glenville Track at East 88th

Samuel Mather

Street and St. Clair.[117] Harry K. Devereux, Samuel Mather's neighbor, was one of the most famous of the horsemen.

Tom L. Johnson, the renown Cleveland mayor, lived in a house on the corner of Euclid and East 24th Street (Oliver). The property had a huge ice skating rink where Johnson entertained with many political parties complete with costumes and beer. The children of the neighborhood were given engraved invitations that said that they were welcome at the rink any time except during Johnson's political parties.[118] Many residents of the elegant homes cultivated the land in back of their homes. Their carriage horses were often used to plow the garden and haul the winter coal.[119]

Euclid Avenue peaked from 1875 to 1900. A famous American traveler, Bayard Taylor, described it as the most beautiful street in the world. John Fisk, a lecturer before the Royal Society of Great Britain in 1860, described the street as

> bordered on each side with a double row of arching trees, and with handsome stone houses of sufficient variety and freedom in architectural design, standing at intervals from 1 to 200 feet along the entire length of the street. The vistas remind one of the nave and aisles of a huge cathedral.[120]

The opening of Euclid Avenue to streetcar traffic at the turn of the century accelerated the growth of businesses and the demise of its residential areas. The street retained its greatness until the end of World War I, although by then the noise of the streetcars, the encroaching businesses, and the influx of immigrants were already causing some of the wealthy to move.[121] Ella Grant Wilson, writing about Euclid Avenue in 1932, described the change: "Tree by tree, the magnificent elms were uprooted. House by house, each one disappeared. The swampy road in 1826 had become the speedway of a thriving community."[122] The old homes lost their appeal as family residences partly due to the expense of upkeep and the difficulty of finding staff. Gradually they became rooming houses and homes for various organizations and agencies.

Charles Frederick Schweinfurth, 1856-1919
Photo property of Western Reserve Historical Society

Chapter Eight

CHARLES FREDERICK SCHWEINFURTH, ARCHITECT

The size and grandeur of the homes on Euclid Avenue attracted prominent architects who were capable of designing and supervising their construction. One of these was Charles Frederick Schweinfurth, who was born on September 3, 1856. His father was a woodcarver who had emigrated from Germany. Under his father's tutelage, he learned architecture, but also carpentry, stone cutting, and bricklaying. These crafts supplemented his knowledge of architecture and increased his reputation as a gifted and competent artist.[123]

Charles and his three brothers became architects, and his sister was a painter. After graduating from high school in 1872, he moved to New York City where he worked for two years in architectural offices. In 1874 he received an appointment in the office of the supervisory architect of the Treasury in Washington, D.C. Schweinfurth married Mary Ella Griggs in 1879. He returned to New York in 1880 and practiced residential architecture until he was commissioned in 1883 to design the Sylvester T. Everett House at 4111 Euclid Avenue in Cleveland.[124] The house, built in a Richardsonian Romanesque style characterized by heavy, rusticated stonework,

Samuel Mather

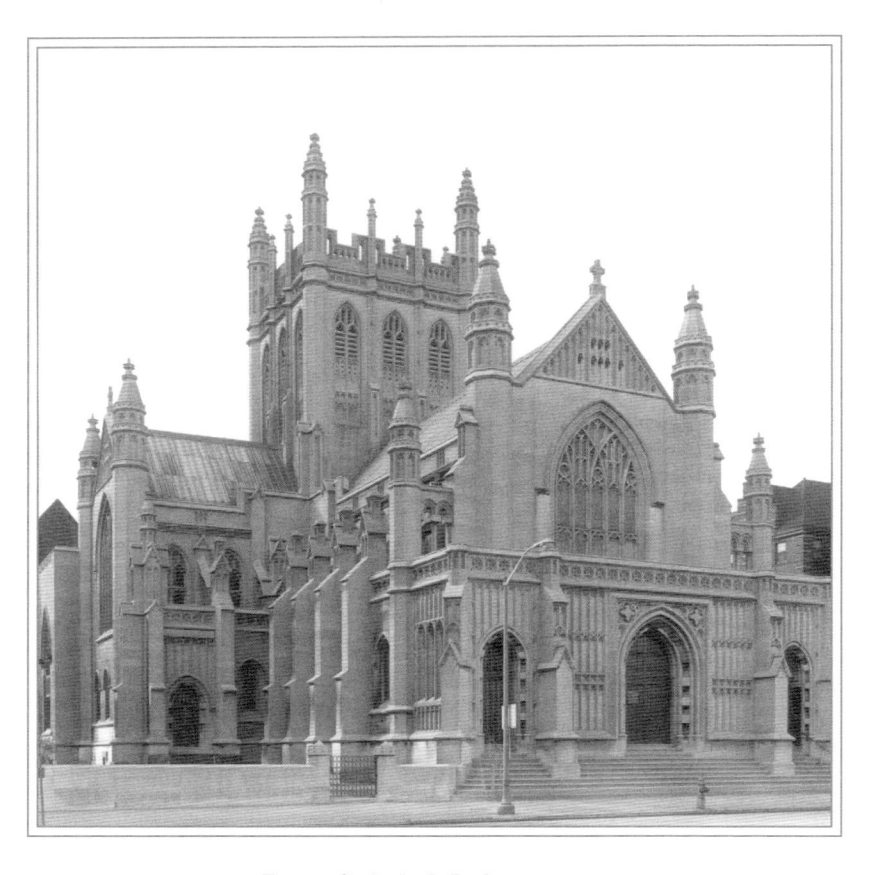

Trinity Cathedral, Built 1901-1907
Photo property of Western Reserve Historical Society

represented the rise of new industry in Cleveland, and was considered to be the grandest house in the city at that time.[125]

Schweinfurth and his brother, J.A. Schweinfurth, settled in their offices in the Blackstone Building in Cleveland and established a practice where they became widely known and respected. They were described in *Leading Manufacturers and Merchants*:

> These gentlemen, although only established in this city three years, have already obtained a substantial patronage in consequence of their previous extensive experience in New York City. Several fine buildings there as well as in Cleveland attest to their knowledge and good taste. Their work was accomplished, not only promptly, but with that intelligent apprehension of design that makes their work highly appreciated.[126]

Schweinfurth designed and built his own home on E. 75 Street in Cleveland and lived there until his death. For a time the house was used as a mortuary, but was later returned to private ownership and remains there today.

In 1899 Schweinfurth was appointed to the Board of Directors of the National Chapter of the American Institute of Architects. In 1903 his first wife died and in 1910 he married a neighbor, Anna Jopling. Neither marriage produced any children. He was about six feet tall with red hair and Germanic features. He was subject to frequent outbursts of temper if he was displeased. Schweinfurth's work consumed him, although he got along well with his workers as long as their work pleased him. He showed no favoritism to the craftsmen. The quality of their work was the only standard by which they were judged.[127] Charles Asa Post wrote, "Schweinfurth was absolutely uncompromising in his insistence on excellent materials and good craftsmanship and possessed an almost complete disregard for expenses."[128]

Schweinfurth lost an eye, although the circumstances of how it happened were debated. Some said it was the result of a quarrel with a plasterer whose work he thought was inferior. As he was destroying the man's work, a piece of plaster flew into his eye. Another story said that the loss of his eye occurred when Schweinfurth destroyed

Samuel Mather

a gold leaf ceiling under construction at the Cuyahoga Courthouse. The workman, furious at Schweinfurth, struck him across the face with a wrench. Years later Philip Mather asked his father which of Schweinfurth's eyes was the glass one. Samuel Mather replied, "Look for the gleam of human kindness; that is his glass eye." Schweinfurth made his own designs and supervised his own work. He felt his life had been a happy and busy one, though at times lonely in his highly focused pursuit of architecture.[129]

There are approximately three periods in Schweinfurth's architectural style. The first is the Richardsonian Romanesque and Shingle style of 1883-1892. Schweinfurth first came to Cleveland to build a home for Samuel Mather's neighbor, Sylvester T. Everett. This fortress-like palace was a reflection of the rise of industry in Cleveland. The second style covers his mature works and the development of an independent style (1894-1900), and the last period includes his late works in Tudor Gothic Revival (1901-1919). The Samuel Mather house was built in this last period.[130] He used the Richardsonian Romanesque, his first style, most effectively in Cleveland and this work was highly influential. Richard Campen writes in his book *Architecture of the Western Reserve*, "He loved massive towers; great entrance arches, rock-faced ashlar (blocks cut in rectangular shapes), mountainous roofs, and towering chimneys."[131]

His interiors contained richly carved woodwork. One of Schweinfurth's most famous works in Cleveland was Trinity Cathedral at Euclid Avenue and 22nd Street, built between 1901 and 1907. Although the original plans were designed in the Romanesque Revival style, Trinity Cathedral was eventually built in the English Perpendicular style of Indiana limestone, sometimes called English Gothic design, with rich detailing inside and out.[132]

Shoreby, Mather Home on Lake Erie
Photo property of Western Reserve Historical Society

Samuel Mather

> It was a bit of a center of worship for the metropolis; it was intended to embody the idea of the permanence of the church; and it was meant to stand as a "benediction" to charity and to humanity.[133]

In 1890 Schweinfurth designed Shoreby, the summer home of Samuel and Flora Mather, which still stands on a bluff overlooking Lake Erie. It was done in his Shingle style, which projects a low horizontal effect, a type of suburban home for the expanding city. Schweinfurth contrasted his materials of gray sandstone and bright orange shingles on the exterior. Today, Shoreby is a private club.

Other important Schweinfurth buildings are the Union Club (1906), the interior of the Cuyahoga County Courthouse (1912), his own house, at 1951 East 75th Street (1894), and the remodeled Old Stone Church (1884). The four bridges in Rockefeller Park, which are well known to Clevelanders, were constructed between 1897 and 1900. Charles and his brother Julius designed them, stone and concrete with winding staircases that lead down into Rockefeller Park. These bridges, although showing some wear, are still stable today.

Schweinfurth was closely involved with Western Reserve University. He built several of the buildings for the Women's College, including the Flora Stone Mather Main Building in 1912, Haydn Hall in 1902, and Harkness Chapel in 1902. Schweinfurth also designed the law school for Western Reserve University in 1892. In 1900 he designed the bridges over Liberty Boulevard to connect Gordon, Rockefeller, and Wade Parks, a project made possible by a donation of $100,000 by John D. Rockefeller.

After working for two weeks in an unheated office, Schweinfurth died of pneumonia on November 8, 1919.[134] After Schweinfurth's death Benjamin Hubbell, a fellow architect, said:

He was known as a man of the highest integrity . . . He was recognized in Cleveland and throughout the country as an architect with the deepest regard for professional ethics . . . There can be no question but that his personality, more than that of any other man, had tended to raise the standard of architectural design and construction in Cleveland.[135]

Mather Mansion, Built 1906-1910
Photo by Kathryn L. Makley

Chapter Nine
THE SAMUEL MATHER MANSION, 2605 EUCLID AVENUE

The choice of Charles Schweinfurth as the architect for his house must have been an easy one for Samuel Mather. Both men's lives were characterized by standards of excellence, thoroughness, and attention to detail. Their aesthetic tastes in architecture were similar. Samuel had known and worked with Schweinfurth for years, including on Trinity Cathedral, and in 1890, he had commissioned Schweinfurth to design Shoreby. Samuel must have been pleased with the results because in the early 1900s, he influenced the Union Club to choose Schweinfurth to design their new building on Euclid Avenue.[136]

On December 18, 1906, a permit was issued to build the house on 2605 Euclid Avenue. The forty-three room house that Schweinfurth designed was completed in 1910 and cost in excess of $1 million. It was likely the most expensive house ever built in Cleveland at that time. It was also the largest house ever built, with an unprecedented scope of design, built on the site of the Jacob Perkins estate which had formerly held a large square-towered house. The lot was 150 feet by 700 feet and stretched all the way to Chester Avenue.

The house directly to the west of the Mather Mansion belonged to

Samuel Mather

Harry K. Devereux, a world-famous breeder of trotting and pacing horses and builder of Randall Race Track. (At the age of about ten Deveraux had posed for the artist Archibald Willard as the drummer boy in the "Spirit of 76.") Schweinfurth designed his house in 1890 in the Richardsonian manner of rock-faced, ashlar, and massive roofs.[137] Samuel Mather bought the house in 1916 and the following year allowed the Red Cross to use it. The house was razed in 1951 to make way for the Cleveland Automobile Club's driving school.[138]

To the east of the Mather Mansion was the Leonard C. Hanna house which was built in 1904 and described as a pretentious Stanford White design.[139] The house contained many rare woods; the mahogany woodwork in the dining room alone cost $5,000 to install.[140] From 1921 to 1957 the house was the home of the Cleveland Museum of Natural History. Leonard helped his brother Marcus run his mining company, the M.A. Hanna Company, especially after Marcus went into politics. Today that house no longer exists; in its place is the I-77 freeway.

A great deal of discussion has been devoted to the reasons for Samuel's building of one of the last great mansions on Euclid Avenue's Millionaires Row when twentieth-century life was rapidly encroaching on that style of living. Samuel himself was fifty-nine years old, his wife had died in 1909 after a long illness, his oldest son was married, and the other three children were grown. It has been speculated that Samuel intended the house to be used as a home for the elderly of Trinity Cathedral. Another story says that Samuel's friends advised him against building the house on Euclid Avenue, but he had faith in the street's ability to maintain its grandeur. Perhaps Samuel hoped that the style of the house would set a standard in architectural style for Cleveland architecture. Jan Cigliano wrote in her book *Showplace of America*, "The architect's scheme took in the entire man-made landscape, covering 2.4 acres of formal gardens, squash courts, and eight-car garage and a forty-three room residence."[141] In the final analysis, no one really knows what motivated Samuel to build the mansion.

The house was designed as a Tudor Gothic Revival. It was Schweinfurth's first example of that style in a residential design. Contemporary tastes of the wealthy in the twentieth century forced him away from his Richardsonian Romanesque and Shingle styles and into the Tudor Gothic Revival style.[142] The warm red brick with the stone trim is characteristic of this period. In England there had been no domestic architecture until the Tudor period. Prior to that, architecture had a fortress-like appearance as a reflection of the constant warfare of the times. The Sylvester T. Everett house in the Romanesque style exemplified the earlier period. The Tudor look was not fortress-like; it borrowed some of its details from ecclesiastical architecture, which was peaceful in design.[143] Schweinfurth's medieval vision was expressed by S.J. Kelley, a *Plain Dealer* reporter who visited Schweinfurth at work: "All revealed that the designer's mind dwelt on days of chivalry."[144]

"Like the mansions of the 80s and 90s, it presents its narrow end to the street with the entrance on the side, and stretches back in a long narrow rectangle originally extended by formal gardens."[145] The house is 189 feet deep, 91 feet wide and 51 feet tall to the top of its copper ridges. The brick exterior of the house was a

> special handmade, water struck brick, fired at Gonic, New Hampshire. It duplicated that used by Harvard University in its gates and buildings. Each brick weighing four and one-half pounds was molded and burned in the crude manner of early brick makers. The bricks are dark, reddish brown, then regarded highly by architects who desired an unusual building ace material. Indiana limestone is used in the trim.[146]

The roof of the house is low-hipped, which adds to the low profile, domestic look preferred by the turn-of-the century tycoons. The facade of the house has a decorative oriel window with Gothic tracery in its leaded panes and carved spandrels. This window opens from Flora's second-floor bedroom and study. A semi-hexagonal bay window, designed with a more masculine look, is in Samuel's rooms on the second floor and the library on the first floor. It is more massive than the oriel window and has an unadorned spandrel and boldly detailed cornice. The asymmetry on the facade reflects the Tudor style; it is not as predictable as that of the Georgian period. The architect designed the elaborate coped ashlar chimneys clustered together in the Gothic style with their deeply cut or recessed stonework.[147] The variegated, decoratively carved patterns on the chimneys were the most distinctive chimney designs of Schweinfurth's career.[148] The south facade sits on a limestone terrace with two sets of bronze-mullioned French doors reached by a broad run of stairs. According to Schweinfurth's drawings, much of the limestone carving was done on the site. He also designed the Mather coat of arms on the facade. Although much of it has eroded, one can still see that the coat of arms has a hand holding an arrow with streamers coming out of rocks. The words "Fortiter et Celeriter" (strength and speed) are carved underneath.[149]

On the west side of the house is both the carriage or family entrance and the front entrance. The family entrance lost its portecochere to a World War II iron scrap drive. The main entrance has a churchlike appearance with a Tudor arch flanked by a pair of Tudor arched windows. It contains double bronze doors with cast bronze grillage in the side and transom lights.[150] The William L. Jackson Company in New York made the bronze entrance doors and used a photograph of the doors and Mr. Mather's name in their advertisements in architectural magazines at that time.[151]

Oriel Window Facade of Mather Mansion
Photo by Kathryn L. Makley

Additional cast bronze grillage was on the back porch that led to an elaborate Italian-style sunken garden designed by Charles Adam Platt who had introduced the formal Italian garden to this country.[152] Platt also designed Gwinn in Bratenahl. This was the first time Schweinfurth had included a formal garden in his plans. It was beautifully landscaped and contained imported statuary. The grandchildren loved to play in the garden when they visited. There was a sundial and fountain at the end of the garden, and a brick pergola stood on the west side. At the rear of the garden was a squash court for men only. It was a sport that was considered too "unladylike" for women to play.[153]

Mather Mansion Italianate Garden
Photo property of Western Reserve Historical Society

The interior of the Mather house is considered eclectic in its style. The entire house reflects Samuel's and Schweinfurth's desires for elegance and perfection of detail. The spaciousness of the rooms, breadth of the staircase, and carving of the wood and stone throughout could not be duplicated today.

The entrance hall is the spatial core, around which Schweinfurth placed rooms of arbitrary sizes and arrangements. It reflects an era of grand entertaining within the home and was one of the last homes in Cleveland built in this manner. Later, architects designed houses in Cleveland in a smaller and less-formal style, intended more for family living, and formal entertaining shifted to country clubs.[154]

The entrance hall, 40 feet by 24 feet, is paneled in English brown oak with a beamed ceiling. Tiles in marble, separated by thin lines of brass, form the floor of the entrance hall. The ceilings on the first floor reach to 12 feet. The linen-fold paneling is Tudor and is exceptionally well carved. Samuel placed the Majolica Italian bust with the "roving eye" here, opposite the entrance door. Sometimes small dances were held on the first floor instead of in the third floor ballroom. Warren Wick spoke of attending many dinner and dancing parties there. To the right of the entrance is a waiting room or anteroom that has a minimal amount of carved wood trim. House staff required salesmen and strangers to wait here.

The grand staircase, 10 feet wide, rises to the third floor of the house with steps with low risers. The surrounding details are Gothic and churchlike with pointed arches and a deeply carved ceiling. The posts and balusters display intricate carvings, and each of the three newel posts is different.[155] Unfortunately, a light fixture designed for the largest newel post has been lost. The surfaces of the hand-carved posts were left rough, while the bottom newel post has a unique design of alternating lions and babies connected by fruit festoons.[156]

Samuel Mather

Mather Mansion, Grand Entrance Hall
Photo by Kathryn L. Makley

In 1914 Constance Mather's wedding party assembled on the second floor of the hall, descended the staircase, crossed the center hall that had been decorated with tall vases of yellow chrysanthemums, and entered the drawing room where the wedding took place. Guests filled the drawing room where an altar had been set up with a white satin kneeling stool. The room was filled with white chrysanthemums, some of which were combined with ferns to form a Gothic arch above the kneeling stool.[157] Connie's brothers Amasa and Samuel Livingston were among the wedding party. Amasa, always prolific with verses, toasted her with the poem:

> Connie Mather, would you rather
> Be in the hills, among the chills,
> Far from your brothers three?[158]

Amasa was teasing Connie about her first place of residence at Saranac Lake where Dr. Bishop was assigned on a tuberculosis project.

Classical Ionic columns, pilasters, and moldings decorate the paneling in the drawing room. Schweinfurth used oak and teak on the floors throughout the house. Artisans constructed the fireplace from Italian marble and carved wooden garlands of flowers above the mantel. Buttons marked "M" and "V" are placed by the entrance and near the fireplace, probably for the maid and valet.[159]

The library, measuring 38 feet by 23 feet, boasts a frieze in the wood dado carved by artisans on the site. Scheinfurth copied the design from Augustus Pugin, a nineteenth-century English architect and writer who was the foremost proponent of the Gothic revival. Schweinfurth kept many of Pugin's designs in his portfolio and used them throughout the house. The W. B. McAllister Company executed the woodwork for Schweinfurth in this house, as well as for many other interiors.[160] James Fillous, a master carver who worked in the house, remembered the hard-to-please Schweinfurth and the ease with which he dismissed workers who did not meet his high standards.[161]

The library was really the heart of the family living area. It was here that everyone gathered to chat and have drinks before Sunday dinner. The adults had cocktails and the children drank orange juice. The dean from Trinity Cathedral might have been there. Bishop Leonard, a close friend of Samuel and a frequent guest, always

Mather Mansion, Drawing Room
Photo property of Dalton van Dijk, Johnson & Partners

preferred to be seated in a stiff chair. After drinks someone gave a signal, and everyone rose and entered the dining room."[162]

A 10-foot Elizabethan fireplace, decorated with high wainscoting, accentuates the dining room. The details in the fireplace bear similarities to the one in Samuel's bedroom. The dining room has an inlaid floor and tracery in the ceiling. At the end of the expansive

Mather Mansion Library
Photo property of Dalton, van Dijk, Johnson & Partners

room there is a raised breakfast nook decorated by a classic marble figure, sculpted by Antonio Rossi of Rome in 1870. Purchased by Amasa Stone, it originally stood in the dining room of their home at 1265 Euclid Avenue.[163]

During family dinners the children sat at a separate table in the breakfast nook while the adults sat at the large table. The children considered it an honor to "graduate" to the larger table at age sixteen, although, according to Elizabeth Mather McMillan, the best times were always had at the children's table.[164] Milliken recalled:

> that they (the entire family) loved games, asking questions such as what was the second highest mountain in the world, and similar puzzlers, but apparently they were well practiced, as they could all answer seemingly impossible questions.[165]

Christmas time was very special to the Mather family. On Christmas Eve the family always went to Samuel Livingston Mather's house on Magnolia Drive for caroling.* Milliken remembered that "I got to attend the Christmas Eve parties often at Liv's house on Magnolia Drive. Mr. Samuel Mather was there and joined in the fun although he was then elderly."[166]

On Christmas night the family gathered at the Mather Mansion on Euclid Avenue. With a lighted candle in one hand and a wassail in the other, each member of the family marched through the rooms on the first floor singing "It Came Upon a Midnight Clear" until the procession ended in the dining room for Christmas dinner.[167]

The sumptuous lifestyle of the Mathers in this home was not possible without a staff of servants. Most of the homes on Euclid Avenue had large staffs to maintain the efficiency of the large mansions:

> Most had at least one man, twenty to thirty years old, who was the family coachman, gardener, and chief butler...
> The two or three female servants, seventeen to twenty-five years of age and dressed in starched uniforms, tended the family's cooking, housekeeping, errands and children,

---

*The house was purchased by Hawken School through a generous gift from Bob and Sally Gries and will be used for outreach programs in University Circle.

Mather Mansion, Dining Room
Photo property of Dalton, van Dijk, Johnson & Partners

really running the house. The butler or cook, chief of the internal hierarchy was responsible for managing the staff and arranging menus with the lady of the house.[168]

By 1880, and continuing through the early 1900s . . . English-speaking Irish immigrants now constituted the large majority of the Avenue's servants even though Germans dominated the city's growing foreign born population.[169]

Internal stresses with the staff were inevitable:

> Flora Stone Mather also felt beset by an incompetent maid and a troublemaking nursemaid; the children's nursemaid fabricated menacing stories about the other three girls in their employ, which caused the cook to leave 'in tears' and Flora to fire the nursemaid. Mrs. Mather concluded that it would be less work to take care of the children herself than to referee quarrels among her housekeepers.[170]

A broad hall runs from the left of the center hall where a Gothic-inspired archway opens to Flora's office. The paneling in her office was probably brought from the Amasa Stone house where she had lived previously. Schweinfurth designed the fireplace with a Gothic ogee arch carved in stone. The fireplace was in the Samuel Livingston Mather house in Mentor until the 1930s, when the fireplaces in the two homes were traded.[171] Flora had intended this room to be the center from which she directed and planned her many civic and charitable activities. The architect executed a very bold casing around the doors. Other designs in the room are a Renaissance shell motif, a rope motif, and acanthus leaves.[172]

The billiard room has a rough, masculine atmosphere. The hand-carved oak paneling is quite old and was probably imported from an estate in England. The ceiling is molded plaster designed in the Tudor manner.[173] The cue-stick billiard cabinets have pilasters that slenderize vertically, and the wooden Jacobean strap work is carved to look like leather straps on the cabinets, doorway, and throughout the room.

Samuel's den contains beautiful wood paneling with built-in bookcases. The workmen carved the fireplace in the Baroque manner with elaborate detailing that gives a feeling of movement. The wall plates to the side of the fireplace once held sconces. More of the Jacobean strap work appears in this room, especially in the pediment of the doorway.[174] From the den, Samuel could overlook his formal sunken Italian gardens.

Samuel was an avid player of whist, a popular card game that was a forerunner to bridge. His favorite companions were his brother William, Henry Dalton, a business associate at Pickands Mather & Co., and Bingham, a friend. He would announce with mock seriousness that he was going to have a "vestry" meeting, and the group would disappear into one of the downstairs rooms to play cards.[175]

The first floor also had an elevator next to a steel vault for the family silver. The elevator was installed when the house was built. The children were not supposed to use it without adults; however, Philip got stuck in it once while playing with some friends and had to be rescued.[176]

All of the family's bedrooms are on the second floor. Flora's bedroom was originally a suite of rooms with the oriel window previously described. A dressing room and a marble bathroom complete the suite. Behind this suite is an expansive sitting room measuring 25 feet by 21 feet with its own fireplace.[177]

Samuel's bedroom adjoins Flora's rooms and reflects his masculine taste. It includes a latticed bay window and a fireplace deeply set into an alcove. Alcoves such as this one with the lowered ceiling were popular in the Victorian era. The wood carving in this room is exceptional. The fireplace mantel contains two pieces of wood cut from the same plank and laid together to match the grain. The mantel has a modification of the traditional egg-and-dart design. The carved detail is crisp and typical of Schweinfurth's work. The marble of the fireplace is cut in a Gothic arch.[178]

Constance's bedroom is expansive and has an elaborate chimney. The casing around the doors is quite rich. Her room contains a mix of styles and is not typical of Schweinfurth's work. The wood fireplace has a very delicate design with a light relief reminiscent of the Adams' style. The bracketed ceiling also falls within the Adams' influence. However, by contrast, the rich Victorian wood moldings around the doors are carved to look like stone.[179]

Philip's bedroom originally had dark wood with a carved mantelpiece over the fireplace and wide grates. Both Philip's and Amasa's rooms have deep window seats of marble. Amasa's bedroom has an intricately carved fireplace with a linen-fold pattern. There are brackets shaped like scrolls supporting the mantel. A Renaissance feature is visible in the acanthus leaf design in the fireplace. The molding contains carvings in the egg-and-dart pattern.

On the back stairway the carved oak spindles are placed closely together, emphasizing the extravagance used throughout the house. The radiator alongside is original and has been placed on a marble base. The hardware on the doors and windows was probably the most elaborate available at that time.[180]

The third floor is designed around a grand ballroom. The casings around the doors in the hallway are quite pronounced. Originally an 8-foot by 5-foot painting "Emigrants Crossing the Plains" by Albert Bierstadt hung here. Bierstadt's love of the early West inspired the painting in Paris in 1860, and Amasa Stone bought it in 1868 for $15,000.[181] The painting now hangs in the Cowboy Hall of Fame in Oklahoma City.[182] The ballroom is one of the most impressive rooms in the house. The room measures 27 feet by 65 feet with a 16-foot arched ceiling. It could accommodate up to 300 people for the many elegant parties held here. It also contains a balcony or a gallery from which musicians played the popular strains of the day for dances. There is a herringbone pattern on the floor while the balcony contains most of the decorative details. The design of the rest of the room is simpler. The egg-and-dart picture molding around the room allowed pictures to be hung on wires on the walls. The columns are in classic Corinthian style. The walls contain paneled wainscoting and were probably painted. The current light fixtures are not the original and date from the Art Deco period.[183]

Samuel allowed the house to be used for many parties other than his own, including those for charitable organizations. One evening Cleveland's elite listened to the Italian soprano Galli-Curci, a famous diva from the Metropolitan Opera. The guests sat on gilt chairs, and Elizabeth Ford later recalled watching Eleanor Squire dozing off, only to wake up to find herself clutching the ankle of Warren Bicknell, who was sitting in back of her.[184]

Elizabeth Mather McMillan remembered a party for teenage boys and girls given by her sister, Flora Mather Hosmer. The guests were given flashlights tied to wands as party favors; then all the lights were turned off. Elizabeth McMillan assured me in our conversation, however, that the party was well chaperoned.[185]

Perhaps the most unusual affair given in the ballroom was a fundraiser, sponsored by the Junior League of Cleveland on December 10, 1915. Headed by Kitty Mather and Frances Eells, the Entertainment Committee presented a program of dancing and whistling. The price of admission was fifty cents, with the proceeds going to the Montreal Junior League for local relief work in wartime. The program consisted of three girls to play the piano; four for vocal music; a play called "Mrs. Oakley's Telephone;" dancing and whistling; and buck and wing.*[186] Though this entertainment is not common today, these activities would have been very popular pastimes in the early 1900s.

---

*Originally, ship captains had the slaves dance the buck and wing for exercise. Later, in the mid-nineteenth century, the dance became a type of tap dance performed by African American men who were minstrels and vaudeville dancers. Shooting out of the leg was the wing.

Samuel Mather

Adjoining the ballroom is the trophy room, which probably contained animal trophies from Amasa Mather's big-game trips to Africa, India, Java, and Formosa.

A part of the maid's quarters on the third floor was used for board meetings by Cleveland State University after they acquired the house. The paneling in the room, added later, dates to about 1900. It is possible that the paneling might have been taken from another dismantled home in Cleveland.[187]

The Mather Mansion is the architectural climax if one thinks of the history of Euclid Avenue as that of increasing size and grandeur. It stands today as one of two houses left representing the magnificent scale upon which those homes were built.** But beyond that, it is a manifestation of the fortunes, ideals, and talents of the men and women who contributed so much to Cleveland's history.

**Today there are just two of the original mansions left on Euclid Avenue. The Beckwith house was used until recently as the University Club. A third house, the Anthony and Mary Carlin residence at 3233 Euclid Avenue, was built in 1912 and later torn down. The Carlin house was the last residence on Euclid Avenue to be occupied in the grand manner of the street until 1950.

Epilogue

Following Samuel Mather's death in 1931, the Institute of Music leased the Mather Mansion until 1940 when the Cleveland Automobile Club purchased it. The Club occupied the house until 1967 when Cleveland State University acquired it for $1,518,000 to be incorporated into its enlarging campus. It was renamed University Hall and has housed the Afro-American Cultural Center, CSU's Division of University Relations, and First College, a transitional and innovative college for incoming students. The history and design of this unique house made it an appropriate choice for the Community Conference Center of the Junior League of Cleveland in May 1978.

Following the redecorating project with the Junior League of Cleveland, CSU encouraged community groups to use the facility for conferences and meetings. However, in August 2011, the University closed the mansion and is presently exploring new uses.

In February 1973 the Samuel Mather Mansion became the first building in Cleveland to be included in the National Register of Historic Places. It has also been designated an Ohio Historical Site and a Cleveland Landmark.

Sources Consulted

BOOKS

    Avery, Elroy McKendree. *A History of Cleveland and Its Environs*. Vol. III. Chicago: Lewis Publishing Company, 1918.

    Campbell, Thomas F. *Daniel E. Morgan 1877-1949. The Good Citizen in Politics*. Cleveland: The Press of Western Reserve University, 1966.

    Campbell, Thomas F. *Freedoms Forums. The City Club 1912-62*. Cleveland: The City Club, 1963.

    Campbell, Thomas F. *SASS. Fifty Years of Social Work Education*. Cleveland: The Press of Case Western Reserve University, 1967.

    Campen, Richard. *Architecture of the Western Reserve 1800-1900*. Cleveland: Case Western Reserve University, 1971.

    Chapman, Edmund H. *Cleveland: Village to Metropolis*. Cleveland: The Press of Western Reserve University, 1964.

    Cigliano, Jan. *Showplace of America, Cleveland's Euclid Avenue, 1850-1900*, Kent, Ohio: Kent State University Press, 1991.

    Cleveland Architectural Club Catalog. Cleveland: The Caxton Company, 1909.

    Condon, George. *Cleveland: The Best Kept Secret*. Garden City, New York: Doubleday & Company, 1967.

    Cramer, C. H. *Case Western Reserve*. Boston: Little, Brown and Company, 1976.

    Goulder, Grace. *John D. Rockefeller. The Cleveland Years*. Cleveland: The Western Reserve Historical Society, 1972.

    Haddad, Gladys. *Flora Stone Mather*. Kent: The Kent State University Press, 2007.

Hatcher, Harlan. *The Western Reserve. The Story of New Connecticut in Ohio*. Indianapolis: The Bobbs-Merrill Company, Inc., 1949.

Havighurst, Walter. *Vein of Iron*. Cleveland: The World Publishing Company, 1958.

In Memoriam, Flora Stone Mather. Cleveland: by Samuel Mather, 1910.

Jollie, Rose Marie, *On the Grow with Cleveland*. Cleveland: Cleveland National Bank, 1965.

Kusmer, Kenneth. L. *A Ghetto Takes Shape. Black Cleveland 1870-1930*. Chicago: University of Illinois Press, 1976.

Mather, Amasa Stone, *Extracts from the Letters, Diary and Notebooks of Amasa Stone Mather*. Vols. I & II. Cleveland: Arthur H. Clark Company, 1910.

Milliken, William. *A Time Remembered*. Cleveland: Oberlin Printing Company, 1975.

New England Historic Genealogical Register. Vol. 86. Boston: New England Historic Genealogical Society, 1932.

Post, Charles Asa. *Those Were The Days*. Cleveland: The Caxton Company, 1936.

Rose, William Ganson. *Cleveland, the Making of a City*. Cleveland: The World Publishing Company, 1950.

Schofield, Mary-Peale. *Landmark Architecture of Cleveland*. Pittsburgh: Oberg Park Associates, Incas, 1976.

Squire, Richard J. *Historical Guide to Greater Cleveland*. Bedford: The Lincoln Press, 1964.

Upton, Harriet Taylor. *History of the Western Reserve*. Vol. II. Chicago: Lewis Publishing Company, 1910.

Waite, Florence T. *A Warm Friend for the Spirit*. Cleveland: Family Service Association of Cleveland, 1960.

Whiffen, Marcus, *American Architecture Since 1780*. Cambridge, Massachusetts: The M.I.T. Press, 1969.

Wilson, Ella Grant. *Famous Old Euclid Avenue*. Vol. I. Cleveland: 1932.

THESES

Coe, Nancy. "History of the Collecting of European Paintings and Drawings in the City of Cleveland." unpublished M.A. dissertation, Oberlin College, 1955.

Perry, Regenia. "The Life and Works of Charles Frederick Schweinfurth." unpublished Ph.D. dissertation, Western Reserve University, June 1967.

PERIODICALS AND MAGAZINES

B. J. III. "Samuel Mather." unknown periodical in clipping file, History Department, Cleveland Public Library, October 1931.

Cleveland Topics, September 27, 1924.

Cleveland Town Tidings, Vol. I, No. 31, October 24, 1931.

Covert, Seward A. This Distinguished Building of Ours." *Ohio Motorist*, January 1960, pp. 13-14.

Covert, Seward A. "This Distinguished Building of Ours," Part Two. *Ohio Motorist*, February 1960, pp. 20-22.

"In Society, Mather-Bishop Wedding." *Cleveland Town Topics*, December 12, 1914.

Johannesen, Eric. "Samuel Mather and the Western Reserve Building." *Western Reserve Historical Society News*, January-February 1977, pp. 2-4.

Mather, Samuel. "Address before Committee on Rivers and Harbors." U.S. House of Representatives, Washington, D.C., January 31, 1896. *Cleveland Chamber of Commerce, Reports of Addresses, 1894-97*. Cleveland: Cleveland Chamber of Commerce, 1897.

"Men of Interlake: Samuel Mather." *The Interlake Log*. Cleveland: Pickands Mather & Company, November 1975.

The Brickbuilder. Vol. 18, No. 11, 1909.

"University Officials Pay Tribute to Memory of Late Samuel Mather." *The Reserve Weekly*, Tuesday, October 20, 1931.

NEWSPAPERS

Barnard, William. "Plan Advances to Save Mansion as Mayor's Home." *Cleveland Plain Dealer*, November 20, 1968.

Colebrook Paul F., Jr. "A Mansion With a Past and Future." *Cleveland Plain Dealer*, October 22, 1967.

"Donations to Fund Continued by Will." *The Cleveland Press*, October 19, 1931.

"Dr. Bishop Dies: Led War on TB." *Cleveland News*, September 29, 1955.

Samuel Mather

"Hunting Hill Estate." *Cleveland Press*, September 27, 1933.

"Katharine Livingston Mather Dies in N.Y. at 84." *Cleveland News*, August 10, 1939.

Kelly, S. J. "A Visit to the Old Mather Mansion," *Cleveland Plain Dealer*, 1940.

Kelly, S. J. "Samuel L. Mather and His Euclid Ave. Residence." *Cleveland Plain Dealer*, 1940.

Kelly, S. J. "Samuel Mather, Jr. and the Western Reserve." *Cleveland Plain Dealer*, July 25, 1940.

Kelly, S. J. "The Old Mather Mansion in 1910." *Cleveland Plain Dealer*, August 6, 1940.

Kelly, S. J. "The Passing of the Mather Mansion." *Cleveland Plain Dealer*, July 27, 1940.

Koshar, John Leo. "Western Reserve Building Was Mather's." *Cleveland Plain Dealer*, April 29, 1977.

"Mather Funeral to Be Tomorrow." *Cleveland Plain Dealer*, June 25, 1931.

"Mather Joins National Fight on Prohibition," *Cleveland Plain Dealer*, July 17, 1928.

"Mather Mansion Offered as Center." *Cleveland News*, November 13, 1958.

"Mather Won Many Tributes in Leading Community Fund." *Cleveland News*, October 19, 1931.

Matson, Carlton K. "S. Mather — Intelligent Humanitarian." *The Cleveland Press*, November 14, 1928.

"Mourn Mather, Hail Life Rich in Generosity." *The Cleveland Press*, October 19, 1931.

"Mrs. Robt. H. Bishop, Jr." *The Cleveland Press*, December 24, 1969.

"Nurses at WRU Honor Dr. Bishop with Degrees." *Cleveland Plain Dealer*, June 17, 1948.

"Old Mather House to Be Razed." *The Cleveland Press*, November 2, 1960.

"Outstanding Points in Career of S. Mather." *Cleveland Plain Dealer*, October 19, 1931.

"Philip Mather Is Honored by University School Alumnae." *Cleveland Plain Dealer*, May 15, 1963.

"Philip R. Mather Dies, Noted Industrialist." *Cleveland Plain Dealer*, September 21, 1973.

"Poor Intern Is Dr. Bishop's Worry," *Cleveland Plain Dealer*, August 22, 1954.

Reeves, Russel H. "Biographer Traces Mather Family." *Cleveland Plain Dealer*, Magazine Section, April 30, 1933.

"Reserve Left 2 Million in Mather Will." *Cleveland Plain Dealer*, December 12, 1931.

"Samuel Livingston Mather Industrialist Is Dead." *Cleveland Plain Dealer*, September 12, 1960.

Sabath, Donald. "Mather Built Home in 1910." *Cleveland Plain Dealer*, February 8, 1969.

"Samuel Mather Gets Award for Community Fund Work." *Cleveland News*, November 30, 1930.

Strassmeyer, Mary. "Euclid Avenue Grew up in Glory," *Cleveland Plain Dealer*, January 21, 1976.

Weidenthal, Bud. "CSU University Hall Given Historic Status," *The Cleveland Press*, February 28, 1973.

Weidenthal, Bud. "Hall Mansion Brings Tradition Overnight to CSU." *The Cleveland Press*, September 13, 1968.

UNPUBLISHED MATERIAL

Hallet, Tom. Press Release. Office of Public Information, Cleveland State University, July 29, 1974.

Milliken, William. Letter to author, June 3, 1977.

National Register of Historic Places Inventory—Nomination Form, February 6, 1973.

Pomeroy, Incia C. "The First Forty Years of the Cleveland Junior League."

Samuel Mather Family Papers, c.1872-1972. Picture Group. Manuscript Collection, Western Reserve Historical Society, Cleveland.

"University Hall." Department of Development, Cleveland State University, 1973. Western Reserve University. Publicity Releases February 21, 1931.

Samuel Mather

INTERVIEWS

    Campen, Richard. Interview with author, June 1977.

    Colket, Meredith. Interview with author, June 1977.

    Fillous, James. Interview with author, Shaker Heights, Ohio, July 7, 1977.

    Ford, Elizabeth Brooks. Interview with author and Emily Brasfield, Cleveland, Ohio, May 23, 1977.

    Gaede, Robert. Tour and interview with members of Junior League in Mather Mansion, 2605 Euclid Avenue, Cleveland, Ohio, June 7, 1977.

    Ireland, James D. Interviews with author, March 1977 and August 1, 1977.

    Izant, Grace Goulder. Interview with author, April 1977.

    Levin, Maxine. Interview with author, June 1977.

    McBride, Mrs. Donald. Interview with Carol Forbes, April 1977.

    McMillan, Elizabeth Mather. Interview with author, June 22, 1977.

    Price, Constance Mather, Interviews with author, March, June 1977.

    Robinson, Alexander. Interview with author, Cleveland, Ohio, June 23, 1977.

    The Samuel Mather Family, A Register of Its Papers, 1834-1967 in the Western Reserve Historical Society. Processed by Raymund E. Goeler and Debra R. Biggs. Edited by John J. Grabowski, the Western Reserve Historical Society, 1978.

    Schofield, Mary-Peale. Interview with author, June 1, 1977.

    Wick, Warren. Interview with Emily Brasfield and author, Cleveland, Ohio, May 2, 1977.

    Wing, Marie Remington. Interview with author, Mentor, Ohio, June 25, 1977.

Endnotes

[1] William Ganson Rose, *Cleveland, The Making of a City*, (Cleveland: The World Publishing Company), The Kent State University Press, Kent, Ohio, 1950, p. 898.

[2] Russel H. Reeves, "Biographer Traces Mather Family," *Cleveland Plain Dealer Magazine*, April 30, 1933, p. 2.

[3] *Ibid.*, p. 2.

[4] William Ganson Rose, *Cleveland, The Making of a City* (Cleveland: The World Publishing Company), p. 38.

[5] S. J. Kelly, "Samuel Livingston Mather Founds Ore Industry" *Cleveland Plain Dealer*, 1940.

[6] Harlan Hatcher, *The Story of New Connecticut in Ohio,* Indianapolis: The Bobbs-Merrill Company, 1949.

[7] "Samuel Livingston Mather and His Euclid Avenue Residence" *Cleveland Plain Dealer*, 1940.

[8] Rose, *Cleveland, The Making of a City*, pp. 522-523.

[9] Elroy, McKendree Avery, *A History of Cleveland and Its Environs*, III (Chicago: Lewis Publishing Company, 1918), p.2.

[10] "Katharine Livingston Mather Dies in New York," *Cleveland News*, August 10, 1939.

[11] Rose, Cleveland, p. 908.

[12] *Cleveland Town Tidings*, I, No. 31, October 24, 1931.

[13] "Old Mather House to be Razed," *Cleveland Press*, November 2, 1960.

[14] Rose, Cleveland, p. 31.

[15] C.H. Cramer, *Case Western Reserve* (Toronto: Little, Brown & Company, 1976), p. 86.

[16] *Ibid.*, p. 78.

[17] Letter from Samuel Mather to Flora Stone, January 13, 1881, Western Reserve Historical Society, Folder 7, Container 2, Samuel Mather Family Papers.

[18] Letter from Flora Stone to Samuel Mather, July 21, 1881, WRHS, Folder 5, Container 9, Samuel Mather Family Papers.

[19] Letter from Flora Stone to Samuel Mather, September 30, 1881, WRHS, Folder 5, Container 9; and August 28, 1880? Folder 3, Container 9, Samuel Mather Family Papers.

[20] Letter from Samuel Mather to Flora Mather from Pittsburg, January 11, 1887, WRHS. Container 2, Samuel Mather Family Papers.

[21] Samuel Mather to Flora Mather, September 28, 1887. WRHS, Folder 6, Container 7, Samuel Mather Papers.

[22] Eric Johannesen, *Cleveland Architecture*, 1876-1976, pp. 49-57.

[23] Johannesen, *Cleveland Architecture*, 1876-1976, WHRS, 1981, p 18.

[24] Rose, *Cleveland*, p. 894.

[25] Cramer, *Case Western Reserve*, p. 103.

[26] Publicity Release, Western Reserve University, February 21, 1931.

[27] Letter from Samuel Mather to Constance Mather, November 5, 1908, Container 3, Samuel Mather Family Papers, Western Reserve Historical Society, Cleveland, Ohio.

[28] *In Memoriam: Flora Stone Mather*, (Cleveland: by Samuel Mather, 1910, p. 137.

[29] Rose, *Cleveland*, pp. 578-579.

[30] Letter from Samuel Mather to Constance Mather, November 5, 1908, Container 3, Samuel Mather Family Papers, WRHS, Cleveland, Ohio.

[31] *In Memoriam: Flora Stone Mather*, (Cleveland: by Samuel Mather, 1910) The Editorial *The Cleveland Plain Dealer*, January 20, 1909.

[32] Elizabeth Brooks Ford, interview with Emily Brasfield and author, Cleveland, Ohio, May 23, 1977.

ENDNOTES

[33] Marie Remington Wing, interview with author, Mentor, Ohio, June 25, 1977.

[34] Havighurst, *Vein of Iron*, p.34.

[35] *Ibid.* p.36.

[36] *Ibid.* p. 2.

[37] Grace Goulder, *John D. Rockefeller, The Cleveland Years*, WRHS, 1972, p. 161.

[38] "Men of the Interlake," *The Interlake Log,* November 1975, p. 14.

[39] Johannesen, *Samuel Mather and the Western Reserve Building*, p. 3.

[40] *Ibid.* p. 2.

[41] Milliken, letter to author, June 3, 1977.

[42] Cramer, Case Western Reserve, p. 103. "Mather Won Many Tributes in Leading Community Fund," *Cleveland News*, October 19, 1931.

[43] Milliken, letter to author, June 3, 1977.

[44] Nancy Coe, "The History of Collecting European Paintings and Drawings in the City of Cleveland (unpublished M.A. thesis, Oberlin College, 1955), p. xxxiv.

[45] Milliken, letter to author; Ford interview with author, June 3, 1977.

[46] Cramer, *Case Western Reserve*, p.299.

[47] Goulder, *Cleveland*, p. 165.

[48] "Donations to Fund Continued by Will," *Cleveland Press*, October 19, 1931.

[49] Rose, *Cleveland*, p.645.

[50] Florence T. Waite, "A Warm Friend for the Spirit," Cleveland: Family Service Association of Cleveland, 1960), p.171.

[51] "Mather Won Many Tributes in Leading Community Fund," *Cleveland News*, October 19, 1931.

[52] Rose, *Cleveland*, p. 824.

[53] J. B. III, "Samuel Mather," periodical unknown, October, 1931, clipping file, History Department, Cleveland Public Library.

[54] Carlton K. Matson, "Samuel Mather, Intelligent Humanitarian," *Cleveland Press*, November 14, 1928.

[55] Havighurst, *Vein of Iron*, p. 161.

[56] Letter from William Hayward to Connie Mather, WRHS, Container 19, January 31, 1932.

[57] Letter from Flora Mather to Samuel Mather, WRHS, Folder 8, Container 9.

[58] Wick, interview with Emily Brasfield and author, Cleveland, Ohio, May 2, 1977.

[59] Milliken, letter to author.

[60] "Samuel Livingston Mather Industrialist Is Dead," *Cleveland Plain Dealer*, September 12, 1960.

[61] Wick, interview with author.

[62] Amasa Stone Mather, Extracts from Letters, Diary and Notebooks, Volumes I and II, The Arthur H. Clark Company. Cleveland, Ohio, 1910.

[63] *Ibid.*, Volume I, p. 148.

[64] *Ibid.*

[65] *Ibid.*

[66] *Ibid.*, Volume I, pp. 200-21.,

[67] Havighurst, *Vein of Iron*, p. 136.

[68] Constance Mather Price, interview with author, May 1977.

[69] Havighurst, *Vein of Iron*, p. 95.

[70] Wing, interview with author.

[71] Havigurst, *Vein of Iron*, p. 46.

[72] Wing, interview with author.

[73] Wing, interview with author.

[74] Letter from Robert Bishop to Connie Mather, WRHS, Container 20, Samuel Mather Family Papers, c. October 7, 1913.

[75] "In Society, Mather-Bishop Wedding," Samuel Mather Family Papers, December 5, 1914, p. 14.

[76] *News Chronicle* article, WRHS, Container 19.

[77] "Dr. Bishop Dies, Led War on TB," *Cleveland News*, September 29, 1955.

[78] "Mrs. Robert H. Bishop, Jr.," *Cleveland Press*, December 24, 1969.

ENDNOTES

[79] Maxine Levine, interview with author, June 1977.

[80] Letter from Philip Mather to Connie Mather, WRHS, Samuel Mather Family Papers, Folder 7, Container 61, August 14, 1911.

[81] *Ibid.*

[82] *Ibid.*, October 20, 1912.

[83] *Ibid.*, June 19, 1918.

[84] *Ibid.*, December 25, 1922.

[85] Havighurst, *Vein of Iron*, p. 140.

[86] Poem by Amasa Stone Mather, WRHS, Folder 7, Container 61, c. August 16, 1917.

[87] Price, interview with author, April 1977.

[88] Alexander Robinson, interview with author, Cleveland, June 23, 1977.

[89] Letter from Connie M. Bishop to Annie Mather, WRHS, Container 19, June 5, 1950.

[90] Letter from Connie Bishop to Philip Mather, WRHS, Container 19, June 13, 1950.

[91] "Philip Mather Is Honored by University School Alumnae," *Cleveland Plain Dealer*, May 15, 1963.

[92] "Philip Mather Dies, Noted Industrialist," *Cleveland Plain Dealer*, September 21, 1973.

[93] Thomas F. Campbell, *Freedom Forums* (Cleveland: The City Club, 1963), p. 17.

[94] Thomas F. Campbell, *SASS Fifty Years of Social Work* (Cleveland: The Press of Case Western Reserve University, 1961) p. 2.

[95] Samuel Mather, Address before Committee on Rivers and Harbors, United States, House of Representatives, January 31, 1896.

[96] Kenneth Kusmer, *A Ghetto Takes Shape* (Chicago: University of Illinois Press, 1976), p. 36.

[97] *Ibid.*, p. 41.

[98] Thomas F. Campbell, *Daniel E. Morgan, 1877-1949* (Cleveland: The Press of Western Reserve University, 1966), p. 72.

[99] Campbell, *Freedom Forums*, p. 18.

[100] Campbell, *SASS*, p. 3.

[101] Campbell, *Freedom Forums*, p. 19.

[102] Campbell, *Daniel D. Morgan*, p. 12.

[103] Campbell, *SASS*, p. 7.

[104] Waite, *A Warm Friend*, p. 171.

[105] Campbell, *SASS*, p. 17.

[106] Campbell, *Freedom Forums*, p. 21.

[107] Waite, *A Warm Friend*, p, 158.

[108] *Ibid.*, p. 171.

[109] "Mather Joins National Fight on Prohibition," *Cleveland Plain Dealer*, July 17, 1928.

[110] George Condon, *Cleveland, The Best Kept Secret* (Garden City, New York: Doubleday & Company, Inc., 1967), p. 141.

[111] Richard J. Squire, *Historical Guide to Greater Cleveland* (Bedford, Ohio: The Lincoln Press, 1964), p. 27.

[112] Ella Grant Wilson, *Famous Old Euclid Avenue*, p. 109.

[113] Rose Marie Jollie, *On the Crow with Cleveland* (Cleveland: Cleveland National Bank, 1965), p. 15.

[114] Condon, *Cleveland*, p. 141.

[115] Richard Campen, *Architecture of the Western Reserve, 1800-1900* (Cleveland: Case Western Reserve University Press, 1971), p. 239.

[116] Cigliano, Jan, *Showplace of America, Cleveland's Euclid Avenue, 1850-1910* (Kent, Ohio: The Kent State University Press, 1991), p. 32.

[117] Condon, Cleveland, p. 146.

[118] Wick, interview with author.

[119] Charles Asa Post, *Those Were the Days* (Cleveland: The Caxton Company, 1935), p. 4

[120] Condon, *Cleveland*, p. 141.

[121] Kusmer, *A Ghetto Takes Shape*, p. 38.

[122] Wilson, *Famous Old Euclid Avenue*, p. 297.

[123] Memorial Record of the County of Cuyahoga and the City of Cleveland, Ohio, The Lewis Publishing Company: Chicago, pp. 743-744.

[124] Regenia Perry, "The Life and Works of Charles Frederick Schweinfurth," (unpublished Ph.D. dissertation. Western Reserve University, June 1967), p. 61.

[125] Campen, *Architecture of the Western Reserve*, p. 246.

[126] City of Cleveland and Environs, Leading Manufacturers and Merchants, International Publishing Co., 1886, p. 109.

[127] James Fillous, interview with author, Shaker Heights, Ohio, July 7, 1977.

[128] Perry, "Charles Frederick Schweinfurth," p. 70.

[129] Campen, *Architecture of the Western Reserve*, p. 235.

[130] Perry, "Charles Frederick Schweinfurth," p. 78.

[131] Campen, *Architecture of the Western Reserve*, p. 234-235.

[132] *Ibid.*, p. 239.

[133] Johannesen, *Cleveland Architecture, 1876-1976,* WRHS, p. 88.

[134] Perry, "Charles Frederick Schweinfurth," p. 74.

[135] *Ibid.*, p. 78.

[136] Wick, interview with author.

[137] Campen, *Architecture of the Western Reserve*, p. 241.

[138] "Wreckers to End Second Life of Old Devereux Mansion," *Cleveland Plain Dealer,* June 27, 1951.

[139] Campen, *Architecture of the Western Reserve,* p. 242.

[140] Wilson, *Famous Old Euclid Avenue*, p. 297.

[141] Cigliano, Jan, *Showplace of America, Cleveland's Euclid Avenue, 1850-1910*, (Kent, Ohio: The Kent State University Press, 1991), p. 196.

[142] Perry, "Charles Frederick Schweinfurth," p. 196.

[143] Schofield, interview with author, June 1, 1977.

[144] Cigliano, *Showplace of America, Cleveland's Euclid Avenue, 1850-1910*, (Kent, Ohio: The Kent State University Press, 1991), p. 197.

[145] Mary-Peale Schofield, Landmark Architecture in Cleveland (Pittsburgh: Ober Park Associates, Inc., 1976), p. 82.

[146] Seward A. Covert, "This Distinguished Building of Ours," *Ohio Motorist*, January 5, 1960, pp. 13-14.

[147] Robert Gaede, interview and tour, Mather Mansion, 2605 Euclid Avenue, Cleveland, Ohio, June 7, 1977.

[148] Perry, "Charles Frederick Schweinfurth," p. 198.

[149] Price, interview with author, June 1977.

[150] Nomination for National Register of Historic Places, *Cleveland Landmarks Commission*, June 9, 1972.

[151] Cleveland Architectural Club Catalog, 1909, p. 34.

[152] Perry, "Charles Frederick Schweinfurth," p. 198.

[153] Price, interview with author, March 1977.

[154] Schofield, interview with author.

[155] Gaede, interview and tour.

[156] Perry, "Charles Frederick Schweinfurth," p. 199.

[157] "In Society, Mather Bishop Wedding," *Cleveland Town Topics*, December 12, 1914.

[158] Wing, interview with author.

[159] Gaede, interview and tour.

[160] Perry, "Charles Frederick Schweinfurth," p. 199.

[161] James Fillous, interview with author.

[162] Price, interview with author.

[163] Covert, "This Distinguished Building of Ours," January 1960, p. 14.

[164] Elizabeth Mather McMillan, interview with author, June 22, 1977.

[165] Milliken, letter to author.

[166] *Ibid.*

[167] McMillan, interview with author.

[168] Cigliano, p. 246.

ENDNOTES

[169] *Ibid.*

[170] *Ibid.*, p. 248.

[171] McMillan, interview with author.

[172] Gaede, interview and tour.

[173] *Ibid.*

[174] *Ibid.*

[175] Price, interview with author.

[176] *Ibid.*

[177] S. J. Kelly, "The Old Mather Mansion in 1910," *Cleveland Plain Dealer*, August 6, 1940.

[178] Gaede, interview and tour.

[179] *Ibid.*

[180] *Ibid.*

[181] Covert, "This Distinguished Building of Ours," January 1960, p. 21.

[182] Meredith Colket, interview with author, June 1977.

[183] Gaede, interview and tour.

[184] Ford, interview with author.

[185] McMillan, interview with author.

[186] Lucia Pomeroy, "The First Forty Years of the Cleveland Junior League," pp. 2-3.

[187] Gaede, interview and tour.